Making Institutions Work

By the same author

1959   THE UNDIRECTED SOCIETY
1965   THE ART OF JUDGMENT
1967   TOWARDS A SOCIOLOGY OF MANAGEMENT
1968   VALUE SYSTEMS AND SOCIAL PROCESS
1970   FREEDOM IN A ROCKING BOAT

Making Institutions Work

Geoffrey Vickers

A HALSTED PRESS BOOK

JOHN WILEY & SONS
New York

English Language Edition, except U.S.A.
published by
Associated Business Programmes Ltd.
17 Buckingham Gate, London SW1

Published in the U.S.A.
by Halsted Press, a Division
of John Wiley & Sons, Inc.
New York

Library of Congress Catalog Card Number: 73–11543

First published 1973

© Geoffrey Vickers 1973

This book has been printed in Great Britain
by The Anchor Press Ltd. and bound by
Wm. Brendon & Son Ltd., both of Tiptree, Essex

ISBN 0 470–90689–8

'We spend the first year of our lives learning that we end at our skin; and the rest of our lives learning that we don't.'

Saul Gorn

from 'The Individual and Political Life of Information Systems', in E. B. Heilprin *et al.* (Eds.) *Proceedings of the Symposium on Education for Information Sciences*, Warrington Va., 1965, Spartan Books.

For my friends in England and America, to whose invitations, incitements, criticisms, encouragements, I owe far more than this book can testify.

Contents

Foreword

I have an unpopular answer to an unwelcome question. No one should read further who is not prepared to question the continuing usefulness of some most sacred cows—and even some sacred calves, for some of the beliefs to be questioned have acquired their sanctity in very recent times.

The question is posed by two familiar but staggering changes of the last hundred years. One is the escalation of our expectations; the other is the escalation of our institutions. The two have combined to make demands on each of us ordinary men and women of Britain which few have begun to notice, still less to accept as valid and inescapable. The question is how, if at all, these demands can be met and at what cost. Since these costs are the price we shall have to pay to maintain the systems which now sustain us *or any viable alternative,* I describe the theme as the price of membership.

I write of Britain, perhaps only of England, because this is the culture in which I have been bred. I believe that much of what I have to say is relevant to other developed Western countries also; but if it is, those who live there will recognise it better than I. So I will leave them to do the generalising.

Everyone in Britain to day, as in most developed countries, entertains a host of expectations which no one held a hundred years ago. The most important of these concern the public 'order' for which we hold our government wholly or partly responsible. This now includes education to the limit of everyone's capacity, the best health care for everyone, employment in an occupation of one's own choice, insurance against unemployment, sickness and old age, a place to live in and a minimum income, whether at work or not. In each of these fields everyone has factual expectations of what will be available to him if he needs it and ethical expectations of what *ought to be* available. The disparity between the two generates protest and demand for change and keeps both sets of standards constantly on the move. A century ago, no one expected any of these things by right of political membership and scarcely anyone thought that they ought to be expected.

We also still entertain all those liberal expectations which a century ago took the place of these positive assurances. We expect them for all and we have raised them to a higher power. They include the right to question, criticise and dissent from all received opinion and to deny the legitimacy of all authority but at the same time to enjoy protection from all coercion, intimidation and even direction from all organised power, especially public power, and also from all the unorganised power against which organisations are designed to protect us, including the killer, the robber, the racketeer, the blackmailer and the sadistic or predatory boss.

A wider set of expectations concerns facilities which are expected to be available to individuals (in both the factual and the normative sense of expectation) even though the individual must personally choose and pay to use them. These include such familiar novelties as the expectations that pure water should be available everywhere for the turning of a tap; light, heat, power, information and entertainment for the turning of a switch; goods and services of all kinds at no serious distance from every door and abundant facilities for travel by land, sea and air. And although this infinitely more varied and accessible menu of facilities has to be chosen, as well as paid for, by individuals, most people have rising factual expectations of what they will be able to choose and even more have rising ethical expectations of what they ought to be able to choose. The right to equality of opportunity, itself a relative newcomer among our expectations, is being rapidly supplemented, if not supplanted by a newer right to equality of enjoyment, which is just what equality of opportunity does *not* provide. And this is associated with a number of other partly inconsistent standards of what *ought to be* the relative rewards for different kinds of work.

These standards of what ought to be are neither mysterious immutable 'laws' nor mere cloaks for competing wants and not-wants. They arise whenever people argue about matters which seem to them to be even theoretically within human control, and they are the means by which we impose and change specific 'order' (or create disorder) within that field. There would today be no sense in arguing that there ought to be more or less rain; but there is plenty of sense in arguing that there ought to be more houses. And so soon as we come to control rainfall, we shall certainly begin to argue about how much ought to fall on whom. The greater the span of human power, the greater the field of human responsibility is deemed to be, and the wider, in consequence, becomes the area in which ethical

arguments can be used. So our expectations of what ought to be
have grown with our concepts of what might be made to be; and
the field for ethical argument has grown with them. The field of
human conflict has correspondingly widened.

In particular, conflicts about who should get what have grown
wider and fiercer as people have come increasingly to win their
livelihood not directly from field and forest, but from other men, and
still more as they have come to win it from institutions.

For these new expectations of what might be and what ought to be
are today directed not towards individual men, but towards very
large institutions of government and business and labour. It is these
which are expected to satisfy both our factual and our ethical
expectations and which are judged by their success or failure in
doing so. So the conflicts of our age tend to be polarised between
institutions and the individuals who depend on them, even more
than between and within institutions. We live in an institutional
environment, interposed between ourselves and the natural environment on which we still wholly depend.

These institutions are as new as our expectations. In Britain in
the mid-nineteenth century trade unions were still criminal con-
spiracies; the right to form corporations, especially business corporations, was a jealously guarded privilege; and the central government had only one rudimentary department concerned with any
internal regulation beyond justice, law and order. The huge edifice
of our institutions, like the huge edifice of our expectations, has been
largely built within the lives of men alive today.

These three types of institution, government, business and labour,
differ in nature, form and function, but they have one thing in
common as organisations. They all, though in different degrees,
necessarily develop both constraints and goals which are not shared
or even perceived by all or, sometimes, any of those who are dependent on them. The larger and more diverse the groups and
interests which depend on them, the more likely they are to see
these institutions as alien entities. So it is not surprising that so many
individuals should view them with doubt and suspicion.

These doubts and suspicions are multiplied as people come to
realise that all these organisations of all three types have become
interlocked in a single system which imposes on them yet other
constraints and goals still more remote from those of ordinary men
and women. President Eisenhower, when leaving office, warned his
fellow citizens that the defence department, the industrial firms
which made weapons and weapon systems and all the ancillary
organisations engaged in research and development in the field of
defence were in danger of becoming an autonomous, self-exciting

system of this kind. He called it the military-industrial complex. The danger is not confined to the defence field.

In consequence the whole idea of large-scale organisation has become suspect. In earlier days the problem of controlling power was seen largely as the problem of controlling powerful persons, and organisation was welcomed as a means of depersonalising power. It now appears that depersonalised power may be even harder to control. In consequence hopes abound for getting rid of large-scale organisation or making it far more responsive to *all* the individuals whom it affects. These hopes, though valid in a very limited field, seem to me to divert attention from the more important aspect of the problem. This is the difficulty of satisfying not the demands that we as individuals make on our institutions but the demands they make on us.

For these demands are reciprocal. If governments, business enterprises and trade unions are to carry out the infinitely more complex functions which our current situation demands of them, then all who serve them and all who can hold them to account or influence them in any way, will have to support them, as well as control them, by an equally difficult and costly effort. The demand falls not only on their policy makers and officials but on every voter, taxpayer, ratepayer, customer and trade union member; in fact on each of us in every capacity in which we can further or hamper their policies. To meet these demands is *the price of membership*. Those who depend so completely as each of us does on our membership of many human systems cannot afford to withhold the dues which they demand and need from us, if they—and consequently we—are to survive and function. These dues are payable not merely in money— though the money dues also will have to rise—but in all the qualities which are needed to resolve or contain human conflict; in responsibility, loyalty and mutual trust; in intellectual effort and informed debate; in extended sympathy and tolerance; in brief, in a dramatic extension of the frontier which divides self from other and present from future. These demands may already be greater than any of us can support. But it is useful at least to enquire what they are.

The answer will suggest what kind of individuals would be needed to live in and manage the world we have inherited, either in its present shape or in any viable shape into which we might transform it. Perhaps we deliberately avoid so painful an enquiry. For even its first steps show that any acceptable future will demand changes in our individual selves, even in our ideas of our individual selves, far more radical and painful than in our institutions.

Two old archetypes of the individual still dominate our minds. One is the romantic, bloodily battling for lost causes; the other is the 'enlightened' man, whose rationality can dissolve all conflicts into calculations. Neither of these characters is fit to live in the modern world. Neither is capable of supporting or controlling the institutions which he needs to support and control himself; because neither is, or aspires to be, capable of handling the ethical problems involved at the level now required, a level equally inaccessible to bombs and to computers. Our expectations need just as cool an examination as our institutions and especially our expectations of each other and of ourselves.

Such an enquiry reveals a simple but terrible dilemma. In an increasingly interdependent world, each of us becomes inescapably a member of many systems, each of which makes its own demands on us, as well as giving its own assurances. These demands conflict. If we acknowledge them all, we have to resolve or contain a mounting load of internal conflict. If we deny any, we disrupt some relation on which we depend. Every human association makes some demand on its members for responsibility, loyalty and mutual trust. We are unaccustomed to respond to, perhaps incapable of responding to so many and such conflicting demands as are generated by our increasing inter-dependence on each other. The memberships we acknowledge fall increasingly short of those we need to acknowledge, if we are to sustain all the relations on which we in fact depend. The conflicts of our day reflect our failure to meet the demands of our multiple memberships.

So we have either to increase our capacity for resolving or containing conflict or to simplify the world (or allow it to simplify itself) by cutting down what we expect of it, of each other and of ourselves to the measure of our capacities. War, famine and pestilence will do the second except in so far as we succeed in doing the first.

If our world is to survive for another generation in any form which we today should regard as worth striving for, I have no doubt that for everyone, what we expect of ourselves and each other will have to go up and that for most of us in the Western world what we expect the system to provide for us will have to go down. The second will *have to* happen, because if we do not ourselves accept it, the breakdown of the system will impose it far more stringently. The first *needs to* happen, both to prevent the breakdown which will otherwise impose the second on all of us, and also because it seems to me to be demanded of us by our humanity. Our human world is an artifact, built of self- and mutual expectations and sustained by human communication, which constantly confirms, corrects and develops them. To sustain this peculiarly human creation seems to me to be a primary duty, as well as a primary interest of humankind. It is the only dimension along which it is meaningful to speak of human progress.

Most of the papers which form this book grew out of a series of lectures and articles prepared during the last three years in response to invitations from various sources in England and North America. They reflect both the occasions for which they were prepared and my own developing views of the issues which they discuss. I have to some extent cut, expanded and re-written them, but I have not attempted to eliminate all traces of their origin. (I am grateful to those who have allowed me to use in this way some previously published material and to those whose invitations evoked it. Specific acknowledgments appear in appropriate places.) The material, re-written as a book, would be less repetitive and more comprehensive; but it would not necessarily be more convincing or easier to follow. The order in which a writer's ideas develop is usually the most persuasive order in which he can expound them. I have, therefore, kept close to chronological order. Every paper is haunted by the antithesis between the developing demands of institutions and the inherent limitations of the human constituents who form them and depend on them. But the emphasis tends to shift from the first to the second.

I have grouped them in three parts. The first four essays are largely concerned with the development which has produced this institutional explosion and alienated its human constituents; with the strange and unstable ways in which our present institutional system distributes earnings, incomes, wealth and status between man and man and allocates resources between present and future and between individual and collective use; and with the effect on this system of incipient checks on exponential growth. The next four examine the links which none the less unite the institutional and the personal worlds and the demands on individuals made by the need to keep these links from breaking. The last three examine in greater detail the ways in which conflicts are resolved and contained and the process and agencies of social learning.

My concern with ethical regulators may strike some readers as unrealistic. It is absurd, they may contend, to expect men either to generate or to obey standards of behaviour so exacting. This may be so. I am not asserting that it is possible; only that it is necessary, unless we are to scale down startlingly our hopes and aspirations.

On the other hand I am not saying that it is impossible. I do not know, no one knows, what is possible in the architecture of human relations or at what cost. I do know that this is the dimension in which human life is built. I do know that our faith in it, even our awareness of it, is obscured by more than a century's obsession with 'automatic' regulators whether supposedly 'free' markets in goods and services, capital and labour or supposedly 'free' interaction of supposedly 'independent', 'self-seeking' individuals in the democratic process. I do know that the regularities which structure the human world are different in kind and in origin from those which structure the natural world, in that they are self-generated by a process in which the human inhabitants of that human world take an active and partly conscious part; and that this also has been obscured by more than a century of effort devoted to wishing away this inconvenient difference. I believe that these influences have blinded us to the role which standards of self- and mutual expectation have always played, should play and will increasingly play in regulating the affairs of men. The basis for this view and its relation to conventional wisdom on the one hand and current psycho-social theory on the other is indicated briefly throughout the book and rather more comprehensively in the last two chapters.

Finally, I would emphasise that the price of membership here described will, as I believe, be exacted from citizens of tomorrow's overcrowded, urban world, whether their political régime is liberal-democratic, socialist, fascist, communist or some still undefined type along this spectrum. But its payment will be felt much more acutely by citizens of more liberal régimes, who are only now awakening to the fact that they cannot preserve their liberties at a price so relatively trivial as 'eternal vigilance'. The future quality of their régimes will be a function of their capacity for those human qualities which this book explores.

January, 1973

Goring-on-Thames
England

PART 1

The Institutional Explosion

CHAPTER 1

The Demands of a Mixed Economy

Western societies, especially America, are economically very rich and grow richer. On the other hand, Western societies, especially perhaps, America, are tormented by political and social problems which they do not know how to solve. Are these two facts connected? Do the mixed economies which make us rich make demands on us which we are not meeting?

I think they do, and I will try in this chapter to say what I think these demands are, how they have arisen and how, if at all, they can be met.

The Institutional Environment

The distinction between private enterprise and public administration is very old; it was familiar four thousand years ago to Babylonian merchants using state-controlled ports and waterways for their private argosies.[1] To this extent economies have always been mixed. But the mixed economy of which Britain and U.S.A., like other Western countries, are evolving their individual versions is very new and rapidly developing; and it deserves the most careful study. For it is making new demands on all who manage institutions in either sector and on all who serve them and benefit from them. These demands are both social and political—terms closely associated in ways I will explore later. However we classify them, they are demands of a kind which we may be biologically unable to meet and which in any case we have been conditioned to reject by a century of economic ideology.

The novelty of the situation arises partly from the fact that the two sectors have become so closely interconnected, but even more from the fact that both have become so highly institutionalised.

Throughout much of the last four millennia, in the great centres of civilisation, the public sector was largely the private estate of a monarch. He was an ambivalent figure to his subjects. To craftsmen, traders and money lenders he was a potential source of regulation, protection, employment and oppression. In Western countries today the monarch has developed into the immense, composite institution of government. Its powers have grown, and so have the fears and expectations of its subjects. These depend on government today more than ever before to create and preserve the conditions in which they can cultivate their own private estates. They also depend on it increasingly for employment. And being more dependent, they have more to fear as well as to hope. Some of their fears are muted or allayed by the institutions of democracy; but these, important as they are, do not eliminate the distinction between the government and the governed. However effective the power of the governed to choose and change their government and however sensitive the government to the (often mutually inconsistent) wishes of the governed, government as an institution stands over against the individual, governed citizen, no less than it did when it was embodied in the person of a monarch.[2] And the demands which it makes on him grow greater in exact proportion to the demands which he makes on it.[3]

Even more important, the craftsmen, merchants and money lenders have also been institutionalised. Their functions are now the functions of corporations, often of enormous size, which share with government the power and the responsibility for making or marring the conditions of life of ordinary men and women. These so-called private institutions are now linked with the institutions of government in a net of intimate, mutual dependence. Even the trade unions and professional organisations, which individual men and women have created to protect themselves against these mighty institutions, have themselves become mighty institutions, often too large, incoherent and remote to win the understanding or the loyalty of their members.

Thus there has resulted a much more intimate mix at the institutional level and a much more apparent gulf between the institutional and the personal level. Both the more intimate mix and the widening gulf are the source of new problems which our recent history has unfitted us to solve or even to see.

Servants and Members

Though increasingly alienated from the institutional world, individuals are increasingly dependent on it, because far more of them than ever before, rich as well as poor, powerful as well as lowly, earn their livings as the paid servants of institutions; and further, because all of them, whether employed or not, depend increasingly on essential services which are theirs only by right of membership of institutions. They have thus come to depend, always as members and usually also as employees, on an institutional environment.

We are still ensnared by an entrepreneurial myth about the way people earn their livings. Two archetypes still hold the field. One rugged individualist wins his own livelihood directly from the earth or the sea. The other wins it from his fellow men by supplying goods or services which they need. Both these characters are usually conceived as young males. Neither exists today, except in the peripheral fringe of employment. The first is represented by a few surviving subsistence farmers; the second by the shrinking numbers of the self-employed in production, trade and the professions. The functions represented by these archetypes are indeed, as they have always been, the only functions by which men in the aggregate can survive on the planet. But these functions have been almost entirely institutionalised. Nearly all the men, women and children in developed Western countries, are *directly* supported not by the physical or even by the social environment but by the institutional environment, as servants or members of institutions.

Membership is the older, the more universal and the more important of these relations; and its relative importance is rapidly increasing, despite the individualist, contractual ideology of the age that is just closing. No one would survive long enough to earn his own living if he were not first supported as of right, over an ever longer period, through simple membership of a family and a political community. The young and the housewives who are not also wage earners form more than half the individuals in most Western countries today. Even in our obsessively contractual societies, these are supported by right of membership, not by right of contract; and the corresponding duties and responsibilities which they owe derive from the same source. Even those who suppose themselves to be self-supporting through their earnings are in fact subsidised from birth to death by a web of services, from highways to currency, from law enforcement to garbage disposal, provided for them *as members* by the political society to which they belong and paid for by them and their fellow citizens in their political capacities.

Even their relations with the institutions which employ them have some of the characteristics of membership and need to have more, if these institutions are to remain viable. The history of industrial relations for the last fifty years has been largely a history of changes adding rights of membership to what was supposed to be a purely contractual relationship—the elimination of casual labour, protection against arbitrary dismissal, the right to consultation and so on.

Status, Role and Contract

When Maine described the birth of the modern world as the transition from status to contract, he had in mind primarily the eclipse
of *inherited* status. In the old world, it seemed, the many were born
to serve, the few to be served. In the new world the right to claim
and the obligation to render service were to be justified only by
the agreement of the parties concerned and were to extend no
further and no longer than that agreement provided. This change
seemed to promise freedom from tyranny of men by men, one of
the brightest promises of the Enlightenment. Few human dreams
have been so potent, especially in North America, peopled so
largely by men and women escaping from the thraldom of inherited
status.

Like all liberating ideas, this concept of individual freedom based
on contractual rights and obligations disclosed its limitations as it
developed. The first to be noticed was the inability of any market,
especially a labour market, to confer any real freedom of choice on
those who must sell or die; and hence its inadequacy as a means to
distribute incomes in ways which would seem morally equitable or
politically acceptable to an enfranchised democracy. The second
was its inability to generate the demand or regulate the supply of
those goods which can only be collectively chosen and provided.
This kind of 'good' was bound to grow more important, relatively
to marketable goods; it now includes the viability of the whole
physical and social environment. A third shortcoming was the
inability of a contractual world to confer on all an assured and
acceptable status, a need which was found to be as dominant and as
universal in a contractual as in a traditional society.[4]

Status in any society implies membership felt by the individual
and acknowledged by his fellows. But a contractual society does not
encourage the sense of membership; and since only membership
gives the sense of status which individuals need, the gap has been
partly filled by associations of the managed and the governed,
notably by trade unions and professional organisations. In so far as
it remains unfilled, it is expressed by vague but highly charged
demands for greater participation but also for greater autonomy for
smaller groups with which the individual can identify himself,
whether occupational, geographic, racial, religious, ideological or
united merely by age group.

To some extent these demands, both for more participation and
for greater decentralisation, can and should be met. They point to
autocratic anachronisms which we should be better without. But

they are also symptoms of a different and deeper trouble much more difficult to remedy.

They focus concern in both public and private sectors on two groups of problems connected with membership. First, the individual in a contemporary Western society is expected to feel a sense of membership in very large institutions, political, economic and social, sufficient to secure his responsible participation not only in current activities but in containing conflict, resolving conflict and mediating change. The trade unionist, for example, is required to make painful sacrifices for the sake of issues which may be irrelevant or even hostile to his individual conditions of work. He is required, even more radically, to re-think his own and his union's role in modern society. How, if at all, can an adequate sense of membership be generated? On what does it depend and of what does it really consist? These are problems of what I earlier called the widening gulf. They are problems of resolving alienation.

But even if these are surmounted—and increasingly as they are surmounted—there remains the problem of divided loyalties. Every individual in our Western societies is a member of many overlapping societies and is required to apply many partly inconsistent criteria of judgment to the problems which his multiple membership throws up. Consider the conflicting demands which large-scale physical planning makes on the countless individuals whose local milieux it disrupts, or those which a call to strike can make on those who are members of the union involved, employees, citizens, heads of families and dependents on an industry. How, if at all, can these problems be resolved? They are conspicuously problems of what I have called the more intimate mix. They are problems of multi-valued choice.[5]

The demands which our mixed economies make on us are the demands of large-scale, multiple membership.

Constraint and Enablement

The demands of membership are ethical demands but they are rooted in the nature of organisation. Every organisation is both less and more than the sum of its constituents. It is less, because its constituents are constrained by the mere fact of being organised; each has some potentialities which it cannot realise within the constraints which the organisation imposes. But an organisation is also more than the sum of its parts, because its organised constituents can do what none of them could do alone—often including the ability to survive. Constraint and enablement are thus inseparable and related; the more the enablement, the more the constraint must be. If we find it hard to accept the logic of this situation, it is because we are immersed in an individualist ideology which should be as dead as the dodo—unless we are to become as dead as the dodo and for the same reason.

Since men tend to notice their constraints more than their enablements, their capacity for organisation is limited by their capacity to tolerate restraint.

This capacity for organisation has always provided men with a double environment. There is an outer environment, which we regard as external to us. It is to be explored, exploited, shaped to suit us so far as may be, 'adapted to' in so far as it proves to be uncontrollable. But it is not something to which we acknowledge obligation or responsibility.

Within this outer environment, is another, formed by that part of the environment (mostly but not wholly human) to which we acknowledge the obligations of membership. These ties were once simple, strong and largely unconflicting—the family, the tribe, the class, the village, the craft. Every one of them has been eroded by the transition from status to contract explored in the last section.

But the claims which we *need to* acknowledge have grown immeasurably. Each of us forms part of many systems, some very large, some overlapping, all making partly inconsistent claims on us as members. And the outer environment which we can *afford* to treat as independent has correspondingly shrunk. We have become aware of inter-dependent relations, ecological, economic, political and cultural, which link the human populations of the planet with each other, with the other animal and vegetable populations of the earth and with its other physical resources in an unstable system, precariously extended in time. The 'natural' environment, once so apparently limitless, has become absorbed into the institutional systems on which we depend for our enablements, including our survival. The corresponding demands are overwhelming.

We can escape them for a while by denying them. And we do. When an individual cannot meet the demands of all the systems which claim his adherence, he secures himself by drawing more narrowly the boundaries of the memberships which he will acknowledge and eliminating those loyalties which are too painfully inconsistent with others. Fragmentations of this kind are widespread and conspicuous. They are not surprising; they are not necessarily pathological; but they are inconsistent with either political or economic organisation on the scale required by today, still more by tomorrow.

They are exemplified no less by the young, in their rejection of all institutional roles and relationships, than by those of their elders who, according to their young critics, have become too dependent on institutional roles to be whole persons.[6]

Political and Social Coherence

It may be that we are biologically incapable of meeting the political and social demands of the system we have created, especially since the time available is so short. If so, the system will collapse and all that depends on it will perish; and human life, wherever it survives, will begin again in conditions more suited to its inherent limitations. We should not allow this to happen for lack of anything we can do; for the loss would be incalculable and the responsibility would be ours. But it is worthwhile briefly to explore the limitations of political and social coherence so far as we can discern them.

Men are biologically social; they cannot develop into men unless they are reared by and among men. But they are not biologically political. The largest systems in which they or their pre-human forebears associated until recent times, so far as we know, were loose associations of families. The huge political structures of our day, with their complex division of function, wealth and power, are an innovation, dependent on capacities of the human brain of which we know neither the limits nor the working principles. So the terms 'political' and 'social' are drifting apart. It is not surprising that sociologists for some decades should have largely concentrated their studies on small groups or that political scientists should get so little help from the other social sciences.

In small-scale traditional societies there was little or no cleavage either between the individual and society, or between society and state. But the course of Western history has so isolated the individual from his social milieu and at the same time so magnified the scale of political and economic organisation as to create a gulf between man and society. The resultant problems are cultural artifacts, the result of two thousand years of Western history. They are no less real for that.

The Containment and Resolution of Conflict

Every on-going association of persons, however small or large, is a system which survives only so long as it can contain or resolve the conflicts which it engenders. Some generate more conflict than others and all may change with time to generate more or less. So the stability of a society—and I mean stability through change, not unchangeability—depends on whether its proclivity for generating conflict is or is not balanced by its ability to resolve or contain the conflicts that it generates.

The basic mechanism for muting, resolving and containing conflict in a society is its system of rule and role. Rules, from formal laws to the subtlest conventions of courtesy, provide answers to a host of conflicting situations; sometimes directly, as by the habit of queuing and the rule of the road; sometimes indirectly by distributing responsibility for deciding controversial matters, legislative, executive and judicial. Within the system of rules, a system of roles distributes authority for decision and makes it both acceptable and effective by defining both the limits of the roles and the kinds of pressure which may be brought to bear on the role-holders.

The concept of role seems to me to be the most important contribution yet made by the social sciences to our understanding of human relations but I think it is commonly understood in too narrow a sense, so I must define at the outset the meaning which I give to it. By a role I mean the responsibilities which attach to a *position;* that is to say, the expectations which others entertain of someone because he is the holder of a position. By a position I mean any more or less defined relation to another person. Since nearly all our mutual dealings take place within the framework of some more or less defined relationship, the concept of role is of universal application. The 'position' of father, husband, son, friend, neighbour, citizen defines the relations of the holder to one or many others, no less than the position of truck driver or cabinet minister or postman. And from this defining of the relation spring expectations which these others entertain towards the holder of the position, whether they know him or not. Where they know him, their expectations are amplified and made more specific. But even in such cases there remain expectations which attach to the position as such. There are things we are entitled to expect of *any* husband, father or friend, no less than of any truck driver, minister or postman and to which we can appeal, if the holder disappoints us. Conversely, there are things we learn to expect from a particular holder of a position, through our experience of him and to which we can appeal if he deviates from them, even though they are not part of the general role expectation, saying—'That is not like *you*.'

A role, then, is a body of expectations which attach to the holder of a position. Whatever the position, the responsibility can be described in the same general terms. It is 'to do what the situation requires from one in that position'. No rule can fully specify what the unknown situations of the future will thus require. This must be left to the discretion of the role holder; and so must the limitation implied by the words 'one in his position'. Hence the inescapable discretion attached to every role. Hence also the implication that every role-holder, accepting the position and its accompanying role, accepts also the duty of playing it as well as he can. He is expected to *expect of himself* that he will meet the demands and accept the limitations of his position. And he is entitled to expect that all who depend on him will trust him to do so and will act on the assumption that he is doing so unless and until the contrary appears.

A role then is a network of self-, as well as mutual expectations; and a society is a network of roles, and works only so long and so far as its members are prepared to act on the assumptions that it implies. It is thus a huge structure of mutual understanding and mutual trust, based on the self- and mutual expectations implicit in all its established relationships. I return in Chapter 7 to explore more fully the innovative aspects of role playing and their limitations; and in Chapter 9 to analyse more fully the techniques by which conflict is resolved and contained. At this point I need only establish the essential characteristics of the concept as I shall use it and its extreme generality.

Sociologists debate[7] how far these systems of rule and role depend on coercion and the threat of coercion by the public power; but it is, I think, undeniable that the main internal regulator of all human social systems is the system of self- and mutual expectations which they engender. It is these which legitimise the role-player's authority within his role and which signal and evoke resistance to any departure from it. It is these which allow each role-holder discretion to develop his role to the extent that those concerned will tolerate. Thus a system of rule and role combines powerful self-correcting mechanisms with widespread opportunities for initiating change. The transition from status to contract was in fact the transition from a state in which positions, with their accompanying roles and status, were traditionally defined and filled by largely traditional means to one where they could be freely designed and redesigned and their occupants freely appointed and dismissed. This is, I believe, the greatest social invention of our culture. It is this which has made possible the growth of our institutions to their present enormous size. And it is equally this which has generated these demands which we cannot meet.

Conflict remains an important regulator of society. It is much more conspicuous in the culture of the U.S.A. than in the cultures of some other Western nations.[8] But everywhere it is ritualised by rule and role, to an extent which is easily overlooked—until the ritual begins to break down. Legal procedures and political elections are conflictual proceedings—each an example of the 'zero-sum game' —but both depend for their effectiveness and their acceptability

on rule and role. The subtlety of these qualifications is partly concealed from us by the inadequacy of the ways in which we have
been accustomed to think of these processes.

Until recently, the most common model of conflict resolution was
a dynamic one, based on mechanical laws; yet everyone knows that
the analogy between mechanical and human clashes is wildly
inadequate, even in the crudest examples of conflicts which are
'fought to a finish'. Since it became respectable to distinguish energy
from information, games theorists have supplemented the dynamic
model with models drawn from the analysis of games strategy and
have analysed situations in which a common strategy may hold the
best hope for both parties, although their goals are different. But
games theorists assume that the rules of the game or at least the
criteria of success remain constant at least for the duration of the
game; and these assumptions seldom hold in the real-life conflicts
of men with men or men with institutions.

The heirs of the Enlightenment clung to the belief that 'reason'
would not only disclose where the 'best' interests of each individual
lay but would also reveal the 'best' solutions whenever interests
appear to clash. Minds obsessed by classical economics generalised
wildly from its findings about the power of a 'free' market to reconcile the demands of economic men. These models too are wearing
thin. Not everything—or everyone—has a price, even if there is
someone willing to pay. A market does not suffice to distribute
inadequate places in the lifeboats of a sinking ship—a situation far
more common than economists have ever been willing to acknowledge. Something more than eighteenth-century reason—still more,
twentieth-century reason—is needed to reconcile the basic interests
of men.

This 'something more' is one of the commonest facts of experience.
The containment and resolution of conflict depend not only on
bargain and threat but also on persuasion. All, though sometimes
unilateral, are usually mutual; and all in increasing measure depend for their effectiveness on the disputants sharing some of the
constraints and assurances of common membership. Mutual persuasion depends on a shared universe of discourse, whereby it is
possible for the parties to enlarge their shared view of their situation,
their shared repertory of acceptable responses, even their shared
valuation of the always conflicting results to be expected from any
course of action or inaction. Even mutual or unilateral threat is
almost certain to degenerate quickly into the coercion or attempted
destruction which it threatens, unless the deterrent costs are something more than the damage which the other can inflict. Conflict
can be resolved and contained within a socio-political system only

if the constituents of the system include all these built-in regulators in sufficient measure. I will explore them more fully later. Meantime I will label them the constraints and assurances of membership.

The Ethic of Inter-dependence

Students of the future commonly allow that it will be characterised by inter-dependence, rather than by independence and that its system of self- and mutual expectations, in other words its ethic, will be correspondingly changed. I have tried in this chapter to provide a basis for assessing what these changes will need to be, if political and economic organisation is to be maintained even on its present scale. Clearly, if my analysis is substantially right, we shall have to abandon the idea, basic alike to the ethics and the economics of the individualist age, that political and economic life is primarily the interaction of individuals, each pursuing his own well-defined interest by bargaining or battle, muted only by ill-defined consideration for those who are conspicuously ill-equipped for battling or bargaining. Instead, we shall have to conceive ourselves and others as involved primarily, both as agents and as beneficiaries, in maintaining a number of institutional systems which are essential both to our significance and to our survival but which depend equally completely on our capacity to resolve or contain the conflicts which they engender—depend, in other words, on our intelligence, our tolerance, our wisdom and our acceptance of some common constraints and assurances of membership; and in this context 'our' means nearly all of us, for very small minorities can wreck any of these systems by disrupting the expectations on which they depend. We have daily experience of the far-reaching effects which flow from interruptions of key services easily engineered by small determined groups which have disowned the constraints of membership—hijackers, urban guerillas, distributors of postal bombs and so on, not to speak of the more irresponsible strikes.

These demands on us, as I suggested earlier, are of two main kinds. Some fall particularly on institutional role-players. The institutional role-player is committed to play his part in sustaining the institution which employs him; but even a single institution is a complex of systems. A minister of state in charge of a functional department of government, health, transport or even defence, cannot make departmental policy without regard for national policy as a whole or implement the policies he makes without the co-operation of other departments. At the other end of the scale the most subordinate manager in a trading concern has to regulate the internal relations which keep his unit viable, as well as the

external ones which keep it effective; and he must constantly resolve
the conflicts which arise between the two. Enterprises in the private
sector have increasingly to take account of constraints and standards
of success imposed by public policy. Government at every level has
to regulate ever more numerous relations by standards ever more
exacting. None of these conflicts can be solved acceptably by
dictation, bargain or battle, unless these familiar forms of regulation
are facilitated by shared recognition of the common membership
from which the conflicting claims arise. The multi-valued choice is
a function of multiple membership of interlocking systems, all with
legitimate but conflicting claims.[9]

Even more intractable are the demands which cross the widening
gulf between persons and institutions or, more exactly, between
men in their personal and their institutional roles. The official,
responsive to institutional standards of success, is increasingly felt
to be thereby alienated even from those individuals for whose
benefit his institution is supposed to exist; yet his decisions press on
them even more closely. The siting of an airport or a highway
wrecks how many individual 'systems'; and will continue to do so,
however much participation and consultation go to its decision.
And contrariwise, how wide is the aggregate impact of the most
personal decisions! The striker wins his higher wages not from the
employer who concedes them but from all his fellow citizens, except
those who manage to do as well for themselves by the same or
other equally destabilising techniques. The inflationary spiral is
liable at any time to burgeon into instability under positive feedback. Yet a free society which had learned to curb it would be one
in which the constraints of national membership controlled personal
behaviour more effectively than most people today would expect of
their neighbours, still more of themselves. Even the instabilities
which defeat us now are only the visible tip of a much larger iceberg.
Most of our ecological sins have not yet found us out. I examine
them later.

So the century once hailed as the century of the common man
proves to need men who are today most uncommon—uncommon in
their intelligence and even more uncommon in their ability to accept
their membership in many systems and to meet its conflicting
demands; uncommon in their ability to enlarge the boundaries
which separate self from non-self and now from not-now . . .

Uncommon, in a word, in their humanity.

Beyond Optimism and Pessimism

Nothing less than this, as I believe, describes the demands which are made on us, both as doers and as done-by in the politico-economic systems which history has bequeathed to us. We may be incapable of meeting these demands; or, if theoretically capable, we may yet be unable to make the cultural change required in the time available. The prospect could not be more dark or uncertain. But to such situations neither optimism nor pessimism is appropriate. The situation is beyond both—as all serious situations are—and our proper response to it was well defined two centuries ago by an American whose utterance will never be bettered. In 1780, while the House of Representatives of the State of Connecticut was in session, the noonday sky was so strangely darkened that some members, anticipating the approach of Judgment Day, called on the Speaker to adjourn the session so that they might prepare to meet their God. The Speaker ruled—'Gentlemen, either this is the end of the world or it is not. If it is not, our business should proceed. If it is, I prefer to be found doing my duty. Let lights be brought.'

More light—not more energy; we have at present more energy than we need. Not even more information; the limitations on human communication are already at the receiving end. More light; and thereby better means to judge between the conflicting claims of responsibilities which will always necessarily be as various, as imperious and as conflicting as our 'rights'.

[Based on a Howard Crawley Memorial lecture given in the University of Pennsylvania under the joint auspices of the Wharton School and the School of Social work on September 23rd, 1970, and published in the *Wharton Quarterly*, Spring, 1971]

Notes and References

1. For a vivid account of this relationship in the ancient world see Geoffrey Bibby. *Four Thousand Years Ago*. 1961. Collins. London.
2. This at least would seem to be the Anglo-Saxon concept of democracy. The alternative view, which conceives an enfranchised people as itself a collective sovereign ruler, expressed in the French revolution and echoed in the constitution of the United States, was described by Lord Eustace Percy as a heresy. (Eustace Percy. *The Heresy of Democracy*. 1954. London. Eyre & Spottiswoode.) But see also Note 8.
3. I have explored this mutual relationship in a wider context in *Freedom in a Rocking Boat*. 1970. Allen Lane, The Penguin Press. London. pp. 129–32. Paperback 1972 by Penguin Books.
4. Colonel Urwick has contrasted the practice of industry unfavourably with that of the armed forces, where rank and status develop in partial independence of actual employment and survive into retirement. (L. F. Urwick. 'Status'. Address at conference held by Institution of the Indo-Pacific Regional Council of CIOS in Tokyo on 8th May, 1965.)

B

5. I have analysed the multi-valued choice more fully in Chapter 4 of *Value Systems and Social Process*. (1968, London, Tavistock Publications; and New York, Basic Books; paperback by Penguin Books, 1971.)

6. See for example Charles A. Reich. *The Greening of America*.

7. See R. Dahrendorf, *Essays in the Theory of Society*. 1968. London. Routledge & Kegan Paul.

8. The contrast has roots too deep and various to try to summarise in a note. It is a legacy, but not an accident of history.

9. The problems I have defined would, I think, be just as real, though perhaps easier to accept, if our organisations were as 'reticular' as modern theorists of organisation would like them to be. To be a member of too many networks is just as difficult as to be a member of too many hierarchies.

CHAPTER 2

Who Gets What

The Primary Distributive System

The way people keep alive has always been of great concern to them.
It has never been a purely individual achievement. No one ever
survived without being supported for at least part of his life by simple
right of membership in some group to which at the time he was
making no economic contribution at all. Some Cro-Magnon bones
in an Anatolian cave tell us that the man they upheld more than
thirty thousand years ago had from birth a withered and impotent
right arm, beside other infirmities; and that he lived to the then
advanced age of forty or more. They do not tell us whether his
handicap as a 'producer' depressed his social status as much as it
would have done if he had been born—equally unsupported by
'property'—in Britain of 1870 or even 1970; but they remind us that
at the point of consumption, distribution has always been a sharing
based on membership.

I shall describe as 'ethical' the expectations which people have of
themselves and each other by reason of some common membership,
whether these are explicit ideas of what is fair or right or 'required'
or so embedded in accepted custom as to be unexamined and even
unnoticed. Varied and changing but never absent, these ethical
expectations determine the extent of these primary distributive
systems and the pattern of distribution within them.

In the thousand generations that separate us from that remote
but not alien figure—but chiefly, of course, in the last hundred, the
last ten, the last two—the division of labour and the growth of
transport, communications, technology and a money economy have
hugely increased the inter-dependence of *producers* and the size of
the system which they together constitute and on which they all
depend, But it has not increased the size of the primary distributive
groups on which an individual can depend for support by simple
right of membership. Rather the reverse; in Britain today this has

been reduced to the nuclear family in its most limited sense, a group far narrower than that which probably supported our Cro-Magnon ancestor. The rise of civilisation, especially of Western industrial civilisation, has produced an extraordinary contrast between the large-scale inter-dependence of men as producers and the small-scale independence of the primary units which struggle for a share in the product. This struggle is powered increasingly by conflicting ethical expectations. Despite important changes in the last fifty years, it seems to me that our attitudes and ideas about the distribution of individual incomes are far too inept even to sustain the huge productive systems on which they depend now and that they will become still more inept over the next two or three decades.

Necessary changes will be the more difficult because the need to increase and renew capital and the need to create and sustain a viable environment combine to make rapidly growing demands on current production which, if they were met, might exceed any anticipated growth in GNP and so would reduce the amount available for personal consumption. Futurists sometimes assume that, because GNP is expected to rise, total net personal incomes, even each individual net income, will rise also. I see no ground for this assumption. The task of readjusting the relative amounts of personal incomes will be harder, if it has to be done at a time when the total available for the purpose is shrinking, rather than rising.

So I conclude that the further economic and technological development of the world, and in particular of Britain, which futurists normally assume, depends absolutely on radical changes in the attitudes and ideas of people already born about the distribution of income between themselves and their neighbours, between present needs and future needs and between collective use and personal use. In this and the next chapter I examine what these now are, what they will need to be and how, if at all, they might change from the one to the other.

The Secondary Distributive System

Outside those primary distributive systems which usually share a common table and a common roof, the products of mankind's growing productive systems have usually been distributed on the basis of claims based on property or on function. I will subdivide 'function' into 'enterprise', 'office' and 'labour'. Under enterprise I include all the activities now commonly called 'self-employed', a significant expression in its novel implication that the normal means of self-support today is to be employed by an 'other'. I subdivide the remainder, the employees, into 'officials' and 'labour', because this ancient distinction, though slightly blurred, is still of great importance.

For completeness let us add predation, to cover those who live by any kind of extortion, and charity to cover the voluntary redistribution of income across the boundaries of primary distributive systems. Property, predation, charity, enterprise, office and labour—these six claims seem to me to cover every way in which primary groups have ever claimed a share in the product of these growing productive systems, except the ways examined in the next section. I will call them the secondary distributive system.

All these ways were familiar in Memphis and Babylon; but they have often changed their inter-relations, their relative importance and their ethical implications. By the end of the nineteenth century, for example, we in Britain had largely broken the immemorial relation between property, office and predation. No public office could be bought; none carried important opportunities for predation; and many could be won and held (though some not easily) without the aid of property. These were achievements almost without parallel since the rise of civilisation, with its wide disparities in wealth and power.

At the same time a new relation had developed between enterprise and property, encouraged by legitimising the limited liability company, which was greatly to enlarge the character and accessibility of property and, in the twentieth century, was to institutionalise enterprise, vastly enlarge the scope of the official and bring organised labour to a position of power.

Consider first the wide category of the 'self-employed'. The hunter or subsistence farmer who supports himself directly from the natural environment 'earns' neither more nor less than his skill, energy and luck suffices to get. This varies with many factors, some wholly beyond his control; but it does not depend on any human judgment other than his own. He can blame no one for his failures and thank no one but himself for his success. He has no ethical claim on nature for a living.

The scope for the 'self-employed' was vastly extended by the emergence of markets. The trader (including the hunter or farmer disposing of his surplus) wins his subsistence from a new kind of environment, a market environment compounded of other men's wants and other men's surpluses. In theory, the market, if sufficiently 'free', is as independent of him as the natural environment. Price is a function of demand and supply, each beyond the control of any individual buyer or seller; its movements are as independent of him as the movements of game. The market, like the wilderness, does not owe him a living.

From this seedbed grew the entrepreneur, borrowing and ac-
cumulating money, buying plant and material, hiring men, selling
products, ploughing back profits—or failing and falling back into
the ranks of the hired, perhaps to try again. He is an archetype of
the nineteenth century but he is many centuries old. In stature he
may range from Henry Ford to the keeper of a news-stall. Whatever
his stature, the environment in which he operates is an environment
of market relations—with the qualifications which attach to the
concept of a 'labour market'.

In sharp distinction from the entrepreneur of any size and any
type, the hired servant, whether high official or casual labourer, lives
in and off a social and increasingly an institutional environment,
effectively interposed between him and the natural, even between
him and the market environment which limits, nourishes and
threatens his employer. What he gets is provided by contract
between him and an employer. The power of dismissal and the hope
of promotion or increased pay are threats and hopes dependent on
the judgment of others, usually identified men. His livelihood is a
function of a specific human relation. If he is dissatisfied with it, he
has someone to blame, someone to persuade, perhaps even someone
to coerce. His relation with it is a human relation, admitting hate
and loyalty, fear and trust, partnership and alienation. It involves
claims to common membership and ethical expectations based on
common membership, inapplicable to the relation of a hunter with
a forest[1] or even a trader with a commodity market. And this relation is further changed when the employer becomes an institution
and the relation is sustained between officials and workers who are
alike employees.

The gulf between the official and the labourer is as old as Egypt.
The official is hired to help to manage the affairs of an institution
or an enterprise. He represents that institution to others, including
the 'labourers' he manages. To himself, as well as to them, he em-
bodies the authority of the institution. He is identified with its
interests. He is often not easily replaced. His pay, however large, is
relatively unimportant to his employer, compared with his loyalty,
his competence, and his knowledge—partly because these qualities
can make so much difference for good or ill and partly because the
total rewards of him and his fellow officials are usually a tiny proportion of total costs, compared with the wages of those who are
engaged by the thousand.

In the days when work depended largely on human muscle power,
it was natural to distinguish sharply between labour as the source of
energy and the staff of officials who helped to direct it. This model of
control has a long history, going back to the days of slave labour.

reticular

It is dyed with concepts of mechanism formed long before self-regulating machines were thought of. It is out of date. But the control system of an organisation, as of an organism, is still hierarchic as well as reticular, and it is made of officials. There is still a distinction between the regulative system of officials, and the general body of workers.

The Tertiary Distributive System

Ever since the rise of urban civilisation, there has been developing a tertiary system of distribution, which acquired a new order of importance with the industrial age. The public power, however organised, has appropriated a growing share of the national revenue and applied it to common purposes by acts of political choice. In Britain today over forty per cent[2] of the national income is so applied to provide an enormous range of services and benefits, from sewers to diplomats, from retirement pensions to development grants. Some are distributed equally to all (roads), some according to need (medical care), some according to poverty (national assistance). Some are distributed in cash (family allowances), some in kind (refuse disposal). Some are 'public goods' which cannot be otherwise provided or paid for (like most roads). Some are to enforce the use of services, such as education and sewage disposal, which serve a public, as well as a private, interest. Some are to mitigate the unequal distribution of incomes achieved by the secondary system or the unequal distribution of life's major hazards, notably sickness and unemployment. All these principles are likely to need wider extension. The urge to equalise income and security is partly ethical; partly an expression of more widely distributed political power; partly an economic concern for expanding mass markets; and partly the recognition that market valuations are particularly unreliable where buyers or sellers are too weak to have real choice. Even redistributions for other reasons are likely to have some secondary effect in equalising income, since their cost is usually spread less equally than their benefits.

Every individual draws from the tertiary system directly and indirectly, in cash or kind or abated price or common services benefits of fantastic variety; and every individual contributes to it in taxes direct and indirect rates, insurance contributions and enhanced prices or in some at least of these ways. The individual balance sheet of 'ins' and 'outs' is too complex to calculate. Most of its items escape notice unless they are paid or received in cash. All of them derive their rationale from ethical consideration, based on common membership of a political society.

The secondary and tertiary systems are intimately connected. Marketable goods, for example, are distributed over publicly maintained roads and their residues are disposed of by public disposal services. Here again the balance sheet is too complex to calculate, despite assiduous efforts to keep the two systems separate. These efforts are themselves charged with ethical implications.

The resources claimed by the tertiary system are increasing today under the pressure of at least three forces which cannot possibly abate during the next thirty years. The first is the need to create and maintain a viable physical and social environment. No one has yet adequately and convincingly estimated[3] the cost of arresting the present rate of deterioration, still less of meeting minimal expectations through three decades of growing populations and industrial activity. This in turn will make increasing demands for capital accumulation and will involve an increase in the real costs of all activities. A further slice of resources may have to be diverted to mitigating the basic needs of countries which are both under-developed and over-crowded; there is no sign yet that this will be offset by any reduction in the growing allocation to defence and allied expenditure.

Apart from this, there remains the question how far the tertiary system will be further used with the express intention of equalising consumable incomes and, if so, what effect this will have on the secondary system. This invites a cool look at the way the secondary system works now and at its present relation with the tertiary system. But I must first revert to what I have called the institutional world and the effect of its new dominance.

The Institutional World

It is characteristic of our time that nearly all of us earn our livings as employees of institutions. The most familiar aspect of this change is the growth of business corporations, not only in size but in their independence both of their shareholders and of their human founders. They have taken over the function of the large-scale entrepreneur and hugely magnified it. They are the main operative institutions in what I have called the secondary distributive systems. They distribute goods and services to customers, incomes to employees and dividends to shareholders; and their discretion over the disposal of the balance is one of the two main determinants of the volume and direction of capital investment—the other being, of course, the decisions of government.

These institutions are managed by officials, vested with the authority of the corporation and constrained by the roles which the corporation imposes. The rise of institutions has hugely widened the scope for employment as an official. The change has had many consequences, most of them beneficial to the quality of management. One, not necessarily beneficial for the future, seems to me to deserve special mention. The separation of ownership from management has intensified in these institutions the in-built urge to grow. It is profits retained, not profits distributed, which increase the power and scope of the corporation and hence of its chief officials. This urge to grow is free from the limitations which set bounds to the ambitions of even the most acquisitive human entrepreneurs, particularly the limitation of death.

Public institutions and their officials have multiplied no less. Accelerating economic growth and the corresponding growth of population have increased the load on all regulative services which government exists to supply. And many of these involve massive industrial and building operations, notably public health and communications. Some of these have been vested in public corporations; others are carried out by central and local government direct. In either case the responsibilities are carried by officials, constrained by roles which reflect the nature and standards of success of the institution which they serve.

The distinction between the private and the public sector is for many purposes less important than the distinction between institutions which recover their costs from individual users and those which recover them from a class of user, generally through rates and taxes. The second make greater demands than the first on the capacity of those who pay for them to value what is provided, both in terms of efficiency and in terms of distribution. The standards of judgment which they involve are at present so ill-developed as to impose one of the major limitations which it is my object to define and explore.

Though user-supported institutions, whether public or private, have much in common, public corporations, even when user-supported (e.g. in Britain, coal, railways, power), are more closely subject to political control, both directly and through governmental control of their means of capital growth. So the contrast between the public and the private sector retains its importance, even though it is not identical with the distinction between the user-supported and the public-supported sector.

A third kind of institution needs to be noted, typified by the trade union, the professional organisation, the club. It is member-supported.[4] It is distinguished from government institutions (which are also supported by the members of the society governed) by the fact that its membership is more homogeneous and its purposes more limited, so that those on whom it makes demands can more easily assess what its services are worth to them and to their fellow members. Among these, history has given the trade union a unique status. No other institution, with the possible exception of the State itself in wartime, has made on its members demands so exacting or developed an ethos so characteristic and so much at variance with the ethics opposed to it—the ethic of 'United we stand' against the ethic of 'Devil take the hindmost'.[5]

The three kinds of distribution with which this chapter is concerned—between individual and collective use; between capital and consumption; and between one individual and another—are largely determined by the interactions of these three types of institution and by the relations of each type with the individuals on whom it depends. Three broad changes have already been noticed.

The first is the growing inter-dependence between all these institutions. Business depends increasingly on government policy, monetary, fiscal, demographic and social, and it is increasingly required to implement government policy in all these fields. Government, for its part, is dependent both directly and indirectly on the buoyancy of business for its revenues and on the co-operation of business in carrying out its policies. Both are increasingly dependent on the acquiescence and even the active support of organised labour. Yet the policies of the three sets of institutions differ radically, in ways which I will explore further; and the efforts which each might make to accommodate the others are further limited by growing tensions between it and its constituents.

The second novel feature is the mounting degree of alienation between people in their personal capacities and *all* the institutions on which they depend. It seems to me a natural attitude among people who have lost confidence both in traditional standards of distribution and in the supposedly automatic power and justice of the market, and in whom neither reason nor experience has yet generated sufficient faith in its institutions to support acquiescence in their enormous and growing powers. Distrust of institutions necessarily means distrust of their officials (however honest) as being governed by institutional standards of judgment and success—as of course they are and should be.

The third novel feature is the relative decline of property personally owned as an important basis for claims to distribution. Property also has been largely institutionalised. In the complex distribution mediated by business corporations, between employees, customers, government, shareholders and their own growth, distributed profits play a greatly reduced role. This is partly because, as already suggested, the value of growth is more permanently built in to these institutions than it can be into any human entrepreneur; and partly because taxation and inflation have so greatly increased the value of an *undistributed* share in productive assets.

To this radically changed world we bring standards of judgment formed in one which seems inconceivably archaic, even though it is less than a century old. In the next chapter I will briefly examine those standards which have hitherto legitimised the concepts of economic independence and of income differentials and their aptitude of today and tomorrow.

Notes and References

1. Even the hunter may come to recognise a mutual relationship strong enough to make him spare female game in the breeding season. The farmer's mutual relation with his land is still more demanding. The industrial age generated still more rigorous demands, even though it concealed them. I have traced this progression into mutual dependence in *Freedom in a Rocking Boat*, pp. 129–32.
2. I take this figure from an estimate made by Samuel Brittan in the *Political Quarterly* for Jan.–March 1971 (Vol. 42, No. 1). It includes all current and capital expenditure of central and local government on goods and services less expenditure financed by charges.
3. No adequate estimate is yet possible since we do not yet know enough about the current effects, especially the international effects, of activity or the indirect costs of measures taken to control them. The total money cost of current and projected programmes is not an adequate estimate. Estimates of this kind are currently of the order of 1%–2% GNP.
4. I have analysed these differences more fully in *The Art of Judgment*, pp. 135–9 (1965, London, Chapman & Hall, and New York, Basic Books) and *Towards a Sociology of Management*, pp. 67–102 (1967—same publishers).
5. There are, of course, other important types of institution, notably the university and, especially in the United States of America, the independent foundation. But I need not examine them for the purpose of this analysis.

CHAPTER 3

Changing Ethics of Distribution

The Ethic of Independence

Attitudes and ethics vary widely within any society at any given time, and they change gradually and piecemeal. Like radioactive isotopes, they decay asymptotically. Wage negotiations, for example, appeal half consciously both to the mediaeval idea of a just price and to the nineteenth-century idea of a market price, even in twentieth-century situations which are even more remote from a free market than they are from a court of morals. Even the concept of a dominant ethic can mislead; for the standards which actually operate are often remote from those which are acknowledged and with which decisions must somehow be squared.

None the less the concept of a dominant ethic, sometimes of two ethics fighting for dominance, is the most useful available to me. And with these qualifications, it seems broadly true to say that nineteenth-century economics and its associated ethics developed two sharply contrasted doctrines about the relation of work and independence, one identified with the entrepreneur, the other with labour.

The profits of the entrepreneur were deemed to be the measure of the wealth he was creating. The greater they were, the more he must excel as a pacemaker in the race to multiply products and to give better value for money. This view expressed a profound faith in the power of a free market both to stimulate and to regulate the supply and demand of goods and services through the mechanism of price changes.

The labourer's wages, on the other hand, were a cost of production to be minimised. The operation of the market in this sector was more questionable, even in the nineteenth century; it was not clear that it would provide work for all or more than subsistence for those whom it employed. The latter was in theory the more doubtful. Although the division of labour, aided by mechanical power, promised indefinitely expanding production, the poverty of life and its procreativity promised equally indefinite expansion of demand. There was some reason, then, to hope that any man able and willing to work would generally be able to earn his living. There was much more doubt about how good a living he could earn. His multiplying numbers and his correspondingly weak bargaining power seemed likely to keep wage earners as a class permanently at the subsistence level, except for those who possessed rare skills. But even subsistence was independence—while it lasted.

These doubts questioned the adequacy of a market to deal with the lives and livelihoods of men. They were well founded. Markets would prove adequate to evoke, distribute and reward new skills which were scarce but expansible in response to growing demand. They would not prove adequate to raise above subsistence level the wages of the abundant or to provide the super-abundant even with subsistence. These problems would need different solutions. Their current solutions are neither satisfactory nor mutually consistent.

Meantime, faith in the market remained dominant, partly because expansion seemed to be far more important than distribution, partly because the market worked well enough to distribute both work and income among those of the official and entrepreneurial classes who still largely monopolised political power.

Its supremacy was least challenged as a distributor of work. Increasing production was expected to increase employment, as well as products overall, even though the path to it was to eliminate jobs by increasing productivity per worker. Luddites and their successors were regarded as stupid, as well as selfish, for withstanding a process which would benefit them all 'in the long run'.

This view was never widely shared by workers, who were usually ill-equipped to face any run longer than the span between two pay packets. It was based on assumptions, such as the perfect mobility and interchangeability of labour, which were never wholly true and which became ever less realistic with the passage of time. It drew a distinction between wage earners and profit-makers which was neither logically nor psychologically acceptable to wage earners, especially as profit-makers became salaried officials. It required the lowest paid part of the population to provide at its own cost that reserve of unused resources which competitive industry needs. Above all, it left them to absorb the main stresses of those slumps which the trade cycle periodically imposed. It became increasingly unacceptable to workers who were gaining more political power with the extension of the franchise and the growth of the Trade Union movement. It reached its final bankruptcy in the depression of the 1930s.

The failure of the labour market to provide a living wage for its lowest paid attracted rather more political attention than its failure to provide full employment. In Britain the plight of 'sweated labour' engaged the social conscience in the first two decades of this century and produced legislation designed to fix minimum wages largely through the machinery of Trade Boards in those industries where exploitation seemed to be worst. The attempt largely failed; the sad story is instructive reading today.[1] And though public regulation has survived sufficiently to do useful work today among ill-organised trades such as the catering industry, it is still regarded as a stop-gap measure. Its history shows, not the difficulty of fixing minimum rates —this was one of the avowed objects and growing successes of the Trade Union Movement—but the conviction, common to entre-preneurs, trade unionists and legislators alike, that the 'right' way to settle them was by direct negotiation between organised monopolists, representing organised employers and organised labour. Though government had a fairly creditable record in improving hours and conditions of labour, it found as much difficulty in encouraging wage increases in the 1920s as it finds in discouraging them fifty years later.

In the early 1930s the future of our form of capitalist society looked bleak even to its friends. It was failing adequately to produce or distribute goods, services, incomes or jobs. Andrew Shonfield, in *Modern Capitalism*,[3] has described the surprise of himself and others of his generation who studied economics in the 1930s that in the 1950s the System should be performing so well, with apparently so little change. The respite had been bought by a complex and far-reaching agreement, operated largely by the State and paid for partly by the State and partly by industry, designed to insulate the individual, especially the 'worker', from the worst risks of being dependent on such a system for anything so important as his daily bread, without (it was hoped) interfering with the dynamics of the System itself. It left the regulation of wages to collective negotiations; powerful unions were now available to nearly all workers whose skills were not sufficiently rare to give them individual bargaining power. Concentrating on the other proved defect of the 'labour market', it expanded many tentative developments into a comprehensive pack-age deal.

Full employment became a bi-partisan goal of policy, which Keynsian economics seemed to bring within the bounds of the feasible. Within this general assurance, individual risks were cushioned by unemployment insurance with wage-related benefits, redundancy pay, retraining schemes and improved old age pensions. Other major hazards of life were cushioned by national health insurance and sickness benefit; and national assistance spread a

job making
profit making

safety net for all below these more specific provisions. All these benefits were expressly described as rights, although the direct contribution of the beneficiary is limited and sometimes lacking.

The State and industry were now in partnership in the business of providing all with 'independence'. And, since work was to remain the principal distributor of income, this meant that job-making was no less important to the System than profit-making or the making of marketable goods and services. But the three were still assumed to be compatible with each other and with the separate system of monopolist negotiation to which secondary distribution was now largely entrusted.

All this was provided (in Britain) by one of the most remarkable packages of policy making ever achieved with something like common consent. But it has weaknesses and inherent contradictions which we need to analyse if we are to assess the future course of the policy and its associated ethic—or rival ethics.

First, it is not yet sufficiently successful to be stable and cannot become so without breaching one or both of two principles on which it rests. One of these is the need to keep the secondary distributive system, with its market mechanisms, sufficiently separate from the tertiary distributive system, concerned with common rights and individual needs. This requires that few, if any, shall receive by way of State benefit more than they could earn at work. So the level of subsistence set by the State is low; and many thousands of workers, when unemployed, draw even less than that, because their earnings, if at work, would be even lower. To raise minimum wages, whether by law or by negotiation, to a level high enough to make room beneath it for a State guarantee of independence at any acceptable level would further raise the level above which employers find it unprofitable to employ the least 'productive' workers. To subsidise low wages by State supplements, through some form of 'social dividend' or negative income tax—a necessary and on the whole desirable next step, as I believe—will radically change the relations of membership and employment as a title to income, in ways which I examine later.

This problem will be vastly increased if technological development further destroys the relation between jobs and work, as I and many others think it will. The 'package deal' assumed, as economists assumed a century before, that more productivity would mean more jobs, as well as more goods, in the long run. This assumption is now questioned. Futurists commonly assume that technology will continue to displace men, even when men are the only superabundant resource.

On the face of it, the assumption seems absurd. Why economise in the only abundant resource, at the cost of those resources which grow ever more scarce? Yet this is already happening for at least three reasons. We cannot assume that as machines multiply their productivity, the men they displace can be absorbed indefinitely tending yet more machines. There may thus be an inherent and growing disparity between producing goods and producing jobs, as distinct from a mere oscillation between over- and under-employment. If so, this could be readily cured if those displaced could turn to work which machines cannot do—to what Norbert Wiener called the human use of human beings. But there comes the second new barrier. Work which can only be rendered by *persons* is bound to grow much more expensive, relatively to work which can be mechanised. If those who offer it are to get an adequate wage from those who want it, they will be progressively limited by the shrinking market of those who can afford to pay. British postmen recently provided a memorable example. So these services will die; would-be suppliers will be without work; and even those who want them and could afford to pay for them will lack the kind of service which might be expected to proliferate when men are the only abundant resource.

This paradox could only be relieved by supplementing the incomes of buyers or suppliers or both. We are experimenting in both these directions but uncertainly for lack of an ethic confident enough to validate such a mixing of the two systems. But even if this problem were solved, there would remain another resulting from the rate of change. Of the workers displaced by present trends, only a proportion can possibly be retrained for industries which will then be short of men. So we must face the fact that the problem of distributing independence and its corresponding status, either by personal earning or by some other means, has not yet been solved even in principle; and that it will grow even less tractable with the increase in the number of those who have no reasonable prospect of employment at what will then be an acceptable wage.

In any case, subsistence is no longer an acceptable independence. Some freedom of choice is expected and acknowledged as a reasonable demand. The lowest rungs of the economic ladder in an affluent society must bear some relation to the rungs above, as well as to the gulf below. Thus the problem of assuring independence is related to the problem of differential incomes discussed in the next section.

I conclude that the support of those who are not 'self-supporting' through the 'labour market' has been carried about as far as it can be carried without disturbing the independence of the secondary system to an extent far greater than is at present acceptable. Yet it will have to be carried much further, partly because those affected will grow in number and in power to make their protests felt; partly because in an increasingly inter-dependent and (hopefully) increasingly affluent society the ethical strength of their claims will be more widely recognised; and partly because we shall shortly cease to believe in the old myth that we have a society in which no man able and willing to work need lack independence through the operation of a labour market.

More fundamentally, what is coming to the surface is the incompatibility between the principles of competition and membership. Competition assumes that the winner is indifferent to the fate of the loser; membership assumes that he is not. For many years rights of membership, increasingly though grudgingly accorded, have restricted the field of competition. Now they begin to question its *validity*. Growing concern for the loser increasingly affects the non-loser, the loser and the relation between them. It begins to affect the concept of winning and losing even in the areas where competition still notionally applies. I enquire later where these humane and necessarily increasing trends are likely to lead us.

The Ethic of Income Differentials

In contrast to the earnings of the self-employed, however high or low, the wages and salaries of the employed are *decided* by some agreement made by an employer with them or with some organisation representing them. There must exist, therefore, some criteria which determine their relative and absolute levels, and determine also the degree of satisfaction with which each party regards the bargain and hence, among other things, its stability. These criteria are complex but not too elusive to identify. They are familiar to everyone who has had to do with the settlement of wages and salaries in public and private institutions.

The employer (public or private) has three linked concerns, with jobs, pay and men. He has to devise a system of positions which in combination will despatch the work of the undertaking as economically as efficiency allows. Each position must be such as to attract a succession of holders capable of doing what it requires; so each much carry a wage or range of pay sufficiently related to the expectations of potential applicants. And these must also be acceptably related to each other.

The higher the position, the wider the range of discretion which usually attaches to it, the harder (usually) it is to fill well and the less are the repercussions of paying more to get and keep the right man. Thus employers are usually more sensitive to cost in the lower, rather than the upper, reaches of their pay structure. So, usually, are employees. Those who aspire to the better paid posts view employment as a ladder and expect more from promotion than from any rise in the pay of a job presently held. And although they reach their ceiling in time, usually by middle age, they do so much later than the majority, who, from very early in their lives, expect no change in their position and hope for betterment only through getting better paid for the same job, either by finding an employer who will pay more or through a rise in the pay of all such positions through collective negotiations. And since they are the less well paid and often the less involved in their work, their concern with more money is the more intense.

So both employers' and employees' interests combine to sharpen the battle over pay at the lower end of the scale.

It is also at the lower end that the market gives least guidance. To be effective as a regulator, a market requires numerous willing but unconstrained buyers and sellers, dealing in a commodity of which both demand and supply are sensitive to price changes, expanding or shrinking as prices fall or rise. Such a market still operates to some extent to regulate the salaries, and in time the numbers of those with rare skills. When demand grows for a new skill, such as computer programming, existing practitioners are offered more in what becomes a 'sellers' market'. Training facilities multiply to meet the demands of those attracted by the new profession and capable of entering it. Increasing supply is taken up by potential demand until something like equilibrium is reached or passed. The 'market' model is far from perfect. Demand is related not to the cost of programmers but to the cost of computer systems, of which the salaries of programmers is a minor constituent. The lags between demand and supply may produce oscillations too violent to be accepted as 'equilibrium'. None the less, market regulation plays a part which is still valuable in regulating and stimulating demand and supply where even one of them is sensitive to price; and it might be made more valuable by improving the flow of information on which it depends.

But as argued earlier, the 'free' labour market has never been acceptable as a means of fixing the rewards or regulating the supply of general labour; and it grows ever less so. The system misleadingly called collective bargaining was the answer of the 'labouring classes' to those economists who could see no way by which such a class could ever earn more than subsistence. The economists were right in concluding that the laws of supply and demand, operating in a free market, would never give unorganised workers more than subsistence, unless they possessed rare skills. Workers were right to organise to escape this situation. But what resulted is not a 'rectified' market system. It is not a market at all. When a single buyer meets a single seller to renegotiate the price of something which neither can do without for long, neither can get elsewhere and both agree not to call a commodity, they are obviously doing something as remote as can be conceived from what men do in a free market.

If collective negotiations are not a form of bargaining, what are they? They may be simply battles; attempts at mutual coercion by threatening or inflicting harm—or rather by matching such attempted coercion by one side against the other side's capacity to endure it. They are always to some extent battles in this sense. But usually they are more than this. They are attempts, though made under the threat of attempted coercion, to reach an agreed application of several criteria, within a framework of agreed limitations. They are thus attempts at mutual persuasion, in which each party tries to persuade the other to apply different criteria or to change the relative importance of the criteria they use.

What are these criteria? They are multiple and conflicting. They are ethical in form and, I think, in substance. First, there is the criterion of absolute inadequacy, explored in the last section. The lowest wages, it is contended, are below the level that anyone 'ought to be' expected to accept as an 'independence'. Next, a wage may be judged inadequate relatively to other wages, because of the greater responsibility, skill, effort or unpleasantness which it involves; or because other wages have changed and so altered customary differentials. Next, a whole related set of wages or even the whole wage structure may be judged inadequate relatively to what it was, because inflation has altered real values or because increased productivity has 'justified' an all-round increase.[4]

All these except (usually) the first are applicable equally to labour and officials. In addition, an individual official's earning may be judged inadequate because of his increased competence within his role, or because his job has increased in burden, difficulty or importance, or because he could not be replaced at his present salary. The considerations which involve rating differences between individuals grow more weighty as jobs grow in importance.

A half-ethical criterion is hidden even within the strike weapon itself. Although no one explicitly argues that men should be paid for the damage they abstain from doing, rather than for the work they do, the damage which a given interruption of work can do is some measure of its importance and supports a half-conscious sense that those who do such work should be expected to put up with less dissatisfaction than others at any disparity they feel between what they want and what they get.

All these arguments are advanced by those who use them as expressing their ideas of what is fair, right or customary. All, with the possible exception of the last, are accepted by employers as valid in character. Argument centres either on their application—for example, on whether a given differential is too narrow[5]—or on the extent to which they are restricted ethically by their repercussions on consumers or other producers or the economy, or practically, by capacity to pay.

These practical limitations are less calculable than they were. In a free market, the capacity of a single employer to pay higher wages is effectively limited by his profits. Wage negotiations are traditionally a means of getting a larger share of profits and are conceived as affecting almost exclusively the employers and the workers concerned—though even in these simple conditions the need to leave enough margin and confidence for investment sets an ill-defined inner limit. Today, capacity to pay is much more imprecise. The demands of capital accumulation are much higher and harder to quantify. On the other hand, higher costs can more easily be passed on in higher prices when they result from increases affecting all competing employers. Yet even costs which can be passed on cannot be excluded from the calculation; for in so far as they are inflationary, they reduce the value of all incomes and benefit the claimant only to the extent—not a negligible extent—to which they can protect him against the depreciation which they help to speed, by improving his share of the depreciating fund, as against all his fellows—except those who protect themselves equally well by the same or other equally destabilising techniques.

An economy in burgeoning inflation is unstable because, in technical parlance, feedback has become positive. Each price signal evokes action which will accelerate, rather than check, the spiral. The contrast with a self-regulating system is absolute. But the situation cannot be reversed merely by improving the flow of information. These factual limitations operate only by being appreciated in an ethical framework, consisting essentially of what people expect of each other and of themselves.

The relation between bargaining, battling and ethical argument is subtle and greatly obscured by the mythology of the market. But I do not think that anyone who has taken part in wage negotiations would question that ideas, often conflicting, of what is fair and unfair play a large part for good and ill in deciding what shall be demanded, accepted and refused; that these ideas change with the course of debate; and that one main object of the debate is to change them. I have mentioned nine; any negotiator has experienced them all.

Nor should this surprise us. All debates on policy, even between members of a board, a cabinet or a town council, aim at choosing some course which will satisfy disparate and conflicting criteria in the least unacceptable way. Underlying the battles and bargains of the secondary distributive system is an immense budgetary exercise of the same kind, which must be contained by some ethical considerations if it is to be contained at all. I explore this process further in Chapter 11.

Possible Futures

The development traced in this chapter defines a problem which is not soluble within our present distributive ethics. The self-exciting market system which has characterised the last two centuries, phenomenally successful in promoting growth, did not provide acceptably either for the distribution of incomes or for the social and environmental needs to which that growth gave rise. So it was progressively supplemented by state regulation and provision and by trade union negotiation. The last round of this sequence has run into difficulties on several counts. Its mounting costs alarm the rich. Its achievements do not satisfy the poor. It erodes the regulators of the market system, provides no adequate substitutes of its own and so has become gravely unstable. The competition of consumers for larger shares appeals to no standards sufficiently agreed to be capable of determining their differentials or containing their total demand; so it starves the growing needs of investment and of collective use and defeats even its own efforts by the inflation that it engenders.

I am concerned here with only one of the limitations which at present make the problem insoluble. This is the pattern of our expectations, by which we judge the shares which we and our neighbours get of the goods and services available, the way we and they get them and the equity of the result, the possibilities of change and the extent of our obligatons to each other and to the future. This is what I comprehend in distributive ethics. Its possible and necessary changes are the most important and the least explored of all those which futurists are prone to examine—more important even than increased economic understanding and much more important than increased technological expertise.

As I write this, unemployment mounts in Britain, whilst growth and investment lag. If confidence were high, business booming and unemployment minimal, there would be more to divide. But there could not possibly be enough to satisfy all the conflicting claims. We may hope that by the end of the 1970s, the economics of the 1960s may look as silly as the economics of the 1920s looked by the end of the 1930s. But even if it does, the new insight will not have relieved us of the need for a changed distributive ethic; it will at best have made the change a little easier. More for collective use and for investment will still mean less for personal consumption and will still have to be combined with meeting a valid claim for a more equal distribution of what there is.

A mammoth budgeting process is involved. Its minimum requirements are that it should allocate enough to the mounting demands of collective use and investment and that it should distribute the balance among consumers in some way which will not generate more conflict than it can contain. These requirements demand changes in the distributive ethics both of governors and of the governed.

The allocation of resources to collective use, necessary to create and sustain an acceptable physical and social environment, is essentially a function of government. But its preconditions are that the electorate shall recognise the need and shall trust its political and administrative machinery to do what is needed. The second is a greater obstacle than the first. Ecological problems of population and pollution, barely recognised thirty years ago, are headline news today. But governments do not yet command confidence in their competence either to decide these issues or to implement the resulting decisions.

The allocation of resources to investment depends on decisions partly of government and partly of business. Government decisions are subject to the two limitations already mentioned. The decisions of business are governed by business criteria and are affected by uncertainties about demand, prices and costs, which in turn stem largely from the troubles which beset the distribution of personal incomes.

The total of wages and salaries and their differentials are determined largely by the interaction of government, business and organised labour. The minimal requirements of a sufficiently stable system are that the total demand shall not exceed the total available; that changes of differentials shall not create more instability than they cure; that whatever procedures are invoked to settle changes shall not be unacceptably costly; and that the end result shall provide acceptably for those not in work as well as for those in work and shall acceptably relate the two. Not one of these four requirements is satisfied today. To satisfy them would require changes in the expectations entertained by the three types of institutions of each other and of themselves and equally in the self- and mutual expectations of their constituents. For these expectations determine amongst other things what shall be deemed acceptable and unacceptable.

If these demands are to be met, individuals both in their personal and their institutional capacities must learn to make and accept collective decisions of huge scope and often unwelcome impact on themselves. This demand will need acceptance not just by a few but by nearly everyone. For very small minorities today can wreck most of the responses required. Its impact will fall differently on three classes which divide our society today and which reflect the sharp inequality in income and security; inequalities not lessened by our relative equality of opportunity.

First, there are those who need not worry about either the level or the security of their personal incomes. Most of these, though they may be assured partly by property, rely chiefly on the fact that they possess valued skills and find that these support them in comfort through the market. Though occasionally in private practice as professionals, they are usually officials of some institution. In the course of their careers they may pass through more than one institution. They are the heirs and beneficiaries of the entrepreneurial class.

Separated from these by an intermediate layer which is increasingly absorbed by the level below, there are those, far more numerous, whose level and security of income has been won by collective negotiation and depends on it. Roughly these include all unionised occupations, including all but the upper reaches of most professions. These do not trust the market; they have good reason to believe that their valuation in it depends on the pressures they can collectively bring to bear. They are engaged in a struggle to maintain the level and security of their incomes, which increasingly becomes competitive with other unions similarly engaged.

Then there is a class of drop-outs, deliberate or involuntary, who cannot or will not compete individually or secure a place on any of the islands of collective security. Some of these are supported as second-class citizens by the state or by what remains of the un-organised labour market. Some live as predators or as embodied protests against the society into which they do not fit. All are largely recruited at the threshold of employment. For as the second class closes its ranks and tightens its hold on jobs and incomes, initial recruitment dwindles. A high proportion of the unemployed have never been regularly employed. But the third class can also be recruited at any time by casualties from the other two.

These are the three classes into which our society, like other Western societies, is hardening. They are clearly incompatible with any democratic solution of our problems. They derive from social and economic facts rooted in history. They will not change overnight simply because those social and economic facts are changed.

But to change the social and economic facts is a necessary condition for a change in attitudes, even if it is not a sufficient one.

Three such changes seem to me especially obvious and important. They are already happening under the pressure of events but they can be speeded and they need to be speeded, because even the greatest attainable rate of change will be too slow for our needs.

One is a more equitable distribution of income. The floor needs to be raised, and transit from the floor to the next level needs to be much more easy and rapid. It is at present the most arduous of all the steps in the climb to relative comfort and security.[6]

Next, this needs to be done without reducing the numbers of those who can even reach the first rung of the ladder of employment. This means bridging the gap between the secondary and the tertiary system which I explored earlier. I believe that this can only be done by using the tertiary system to subsidise the secondary to a much greater extent than it does now, a change opposed to deeply rooted ideological preconceptions.

A corollary of this levelling up is that higher incomes should be arrested or reduced in real terms. This will affect the whole upper half of the wage-salary structure. The top ten per cent is economically far too small to release the necessary resources, though its psychological importance will demand from it larger sacrifices than from the rest. The only means to this equalisation, within our present system, is, of course, much higher and more steeply graded taxation of incomes or wealth or both. To suppose that it can be done merely by a skewed distribution of the proceeds of growth is mere wishful thinking.[7]

It will be objected that this will reduce incentive. This popular myth has a long history but is supported by no contemporary evidence.[8] In any case, even if it were true, it would be no valid objection. For if incentive merely means discontent, this is exactly what we want to reduce. Why encourage discontent, when for nearly everyone the only way to relieve it is not to work harder but to fight harder?[9]

If we want enough individuals to concern themselves sufficiently with their fellows, their society and its future, we must relieve them sufficiently of their anxieties about self and now.

In adjusting these inequities, it is important that the facts of present equality and inequality should be better known and more fully accepted. Because the relation between the secondary and the tertiary systems is so complex, it is almost impossible for a man to estimate even for himself the contributions that he makes and the benefits he receives. As the teritiary system grows in importance, it becomes ever more important to make clear where the burdens and the benefits are falling. This in turn involves distinguishing inequalities of wealth from inequalities of income. In this chapter I have been little concerned with claims based on property. But the changing role and character of property and the changing routes to acquiring it remain even more important to the distribution of security than of income.

A further necessary but not sufficient condition is a shift of attention and emphasis from the enjoyment and security that can be bought individually to that which can only be bought collectively. This may seem both vague and unlikely; yet it is, I think, particularly easy both to predict and to envisage. For it is the most certain and speedy result of any of the catastrophes which the present trends are set to produce. In war, extreme inflation or other national emergency, prosperity, security, even survival are seen to be attainable only as a collective achievement. In collective, as in individual life, imminent destruction wonderfully clears the mind. Unhappily, it also limits the initiative.

As a basis for anything more than crisis reaction, collective achievements would have to be a source of satisfaction not only in disaster. Our institutions and their achievements have been a source of national pride and international envy when they were neither so efficient nor so equitable as they are now. They might and should be so again.

For distributive ethics are not the whole of ethics. They monopolise attention only when collective goals cease to inspire the vision and faith needed to achieve them. The institutional world of the next generation, if good enough to keep that generation and its successors afloat, will be a human achievement meriting loyalty and dedication as fully as any past flowering of civilisation and promising far more satisfaction than can be drawn from more equitable distribution, even though that will be one of the criteria by which it should be judged, as well as one of the conditions which will make it possible.

No hope could be further from the dominant ethic of today. For years the authority of all the institutions and of their official role-holders has been suspect or rejected by their constituents to the verge of paranoia—and beyond. Role has become a dirty word. But this rejection of the institutional world is not, I believe, a defence of human personality, as is usually pretended, but a rejection of the new demands on human personality which that world is making. These demands require individuals not to reject but to reconcile their institutional loyalties to an extent never before achieved. The responses they require are not subhuman, still less inhuman; and it is not for us to say they are superhuman, merely because we are too scared even to try to achieve them.

[This and the previous chapter first appeared in *Futures*, June 1971, Vol. 3, No. 2. They have been slightly revised.]

Notes and References

1. See for example J. Hallsworth, *The Legal Minimum*, 1925. London. The Labour Publishing Company.
2. It is significant that a society still devoted to preserving competition in the provision of goods and services should favour and encourage monopolist negotiation for the determination of wages. There could be no clearer acknowledgment of the difference between the two situations.
3. Andrew Shonfield, *Modern Capitalism*, 1965. London. O.U.P.
4. This universally accepted justification is in fact a monstrous imposition. Those whose productivity is increased by machines which they have neither bought nor invented have no ethical claim whatever to benefit from the improvement except as consumers, through the reduction in costs of living which would accrue to all if increased productivity were passed on to all in reduction of price.
5. Techniques of job evaluation have developed empirically, with little basic understanding of the criteria which people actually use in judging differentials. Professor Elliott Jacques, in 1955, found remarkable agreement within one firm and equated it with a factor which he called the time-span of responsibility, a measure which has gained some acceptance. But the research on which it was based has not, I think, been repeated. (Elliott Jacques, *Measurement of Responsibility*, 1956, London Tavistock Publications, and *Equitable Payment*, 1961, London, Heinemann and [revised] 1967 Penguin Books.)
6. David Piachaud in an article on Poverty and Taxation in the *Political Quarterly* already quoted (Jan.–March 1971, Vol. 42, No. 1) points out that a four-child family in Britain which (at that time) increased its earnings from £20 to £23 a week was better off by only 4/–, a marginal tax rate of 93 per cent, which is more severe than that applicable at £50,000 a year. The example, though extreme, illustrates the way in which the present incidence of benefits confined to 'the poor', such as free school meals, creates a barrier round the class which they define.
7. David Piachaud, in the article already quoted, points out that to add £1 per week net to the income of all who were then at or below two-thirds of the national average would require an increase of 2/9d in the pound in the standard rate of tax. Even so, everyone earning up to £27 a week would benefit.
8. Maurice Peston, in an article on *Incentives, Distortion and the System of Taxation* in the *Political Quarterly* already quoted (Jan.–March 1971, Vol. 42, No. 1), discusses the infinite variety of impact which tax changes may have on individuals; but testifies that he never met anyone who did not believe that higher rates were a disincentive *to others* and equally never met anyone who would admit that they were a disincentive *to him*.
9. The whole concept of incentives is distorted by two historic concepts; the labourer on piece-work goaded to overwork to keep alive; and the entrepreneur with an insatiable lust to make a fortune. Neither is typical today. Neither has any place in any viable tomorrow.

CHAPTER 4

Towards a More Stable State

Global Forecasts—Their Uses and Limitations.

It is widely repeated, though not yet widely believed, that the presently rising trends in economic production and still more in individual affluence will be checked and perhaps reversed within a few decades by the interaction of five factors[1]—the depletion of metals and minerals; the depletion of fossil fuels; pollution; increasing populations; and the limitations of bio-synthesis, notably in their effect on food production. Conflicting forecasts based on these trends are engendering controversy more suited to a religious heresy than a scientific debate. This should be resisted; for it diverts attention from what should be today a concerted intellectual effort.

The argument between ecodoomsters and their critics is serving an invaluable purpose by making *debatable* what had before been taken for granted. It should not need a computer to persuade an intelligent person that a bounded system cannot expand indefinitely. But computer-based arguments usefully demonstrate how quickly such limitations might begin to hurt and how illusory piecemeal remedies might be.

The trouble with the ecodoomsters' arguments is that, at present, they are both too precise and too general for most purposes. A demonstration made on the basis of *any* assumptions precise enough to be computerised raises arguments about the validity of the assumptions. And however wide the variety of alternative assumptions used, it cannot be *proved* that they are wide enough to bracket the whole field of the possible. On the other hand, world models using variables so general as those used by Professors Forrester and Meadows are too general to pose problems with the precision needed by particular policy making bodies here and now, notably by the central governments of political states which are today, with all their defects, by far the most potent general regulators on the planet and are likely to remain so during the critical two or three decades ahead.

So I regard the present round of global forecasting as a potent and welcome exercise in the education of both governors and governed, likely to produce three changes which are greatly to be welcomed. First, it should teach us to understand better the systems which governments exist to regulate and so the nature of government and of the demands it makes on all of us. Secondly, it should make us all more aware of the limitations of our planet as a whole and the impact of these on national policies. Thirdly, it should develop a powerful instrument for working out the implications of any set of assumptions and consequently should focus attention on what those assumptions ought to be.

But while all this is going on, there are policy decisions to be taken; and the questions to which policy makers need answers for their present purposes are not necessarily those about which technological forecasters are arguing. In this chapter I make a brief survey of the issues raised by the forecasters and try to extract from them those conclusions bearing on or calling for present British policy making which need not wait for the forecasters to reach agreement or which require forecasts more specific than those about which they are arguing.

The five factors already mentioned, though closely related, are partly independent. The forecasters rightly stress their interconnection and the inadequacy of policies directed to any one of them. None the less, policies as they emerge in Acts of Parliament or executive action, are necessarily specific. It is useful to look at each of the five fields separately and enquire what action each invites now and what further information each requires now in the specific context of Britain.

But first it should be acknowledged that the five factors working together form a powerful force tending *towards a more stable state* of relations between men and their physical home.

The Meaning of Stability

The term 'steady state' has been so grossly misused that no useful discussion can take place until the concept of stability has been rescued from its present confusion and given a more precise and realistic meaning.

A man who claimed that his finances had always been in a steady state would be saying nothing about his income or his expenditure but only something about the relation between them. He would be asserting, first, that the outflow had never exceeded the inflow except by amounts which could be covered by his capital or bridged by repayable loans. The volume of the flow need not have been in the least constant; what remained steady had been the relation between them, as he progressed perhaps from penurious clerk to millionaire.

Even this is a meaning more subtle than most people associate with steady state. Yet had he meant no more than that, his statement would have been a mere tautology. Outflow *cannot* exceed inflow. If food fails, people starve and die. In a money economy they starve and die if they lack money, even though food be plentiful, unless some larger social system covers their deficiency from its abundance. The stability which the prudent man claims to have maintained must be more than that which necessity would have forced on him; and so it is. He is claiming success in having adjusted his commitments to his resources with sufficient prescience to realise his intentions within the limit of his means, without constant loss and frustration through the shortfall of resources when they were needed.

Stability is thus a very modest *criterion* of financial success. We are more prone to measure financial success either by the amount of money a man makes or by the effect he produces by the way he spends it. Stability, however, though modest as a *criterion*, is crucial as a *condition* of success. Without adequate skill in preserving stability, it is hard for a man either to accumulate wealth or to do anything striking with it, either for good or ill.

The economy of a business, a city or a nation state measures its stability in the same way. The deliberations of those who direct it may be largely concerned with how to increase its income and how to apportion it between rival uses, the demands of which always exceed its total amount. But in the background are controllers who are concerned to see that total commitments, however good their purpose, do not exceed total resources. And much policy making is concerned with determining what these limits, never precisely predictable, shall be assumed to be. Too cautious an approach leaves resources unnecessarily sterilised; but too rash a policy may waste enormous investment already committed and rob the policy maker of any initiative for years to come.

These considerations can all be applied equally to the planet as a whole. We have not felt the need to do so in the past. Even today most of our practical thinking needs to be done in terms of smaller units. But the planetary background is growing ever more important and is not so widely appreciated as it needs to be.

The Stability of Material Supply

The planet, unlike the human individual, has a guaranteed income in the sun's energy. It has also a capacity which is not guaranteed but which has not previously been called in question to build from this base the huge architecture of organic life, which until very recently supported our species without our co-operation, as ultimate parasites, browsing on the topmost links of innumerable food chains. This process of biosynthesis which I will call the natural productive process employs no labour, costs no money, causes no pollution, upgrades everything it touches and provides mankind with his food and much of the materials he uses, usually far more complex in structure and composition than any which his factories can produce. Since the agricultural epoch began, men have intervened in this process to elicit from it more of what they wanted where they wanted it. During the industrial age, men increased and used their powers of processing and distributing. In its latest stages they have begun to convert material, including natural products, into new materials more convenient to their purposes. But the natural productive process still far over-shadows the human activity of conversion.

This human involvement with the natural productive process has been made possible by drawing on metals and minerals for tools and on fossil fuels for power. Neither of these resources is regenerated by the natural productive process, and both are consumed by use though at different rates. They form a relatively small proportion of the resources consumed annually by men; but because of the key role they play and the fact that they are not naturally regenerated, it would be crazy not to examine their known supplies, the rate at which they are being consumed and the possibility of replacing them with less rare substitutes. And in estimating the possibilities of substitution it is useful to distinguish materials used for tools and machines from those used for other purposes. Materials of which the end products are used for human consumption are largely produced by or from the natural productive process and those which are not so derived now could perhaps be replaced by products converted from a natural base. But our dependence on metals for tools and machines has so far been almost complete and the prospect of replacing these by naturally regenerated products is both more remote and, I understand, much less sure.

If this were all, it would be time to give some thought internationally and still more within the context of some national economies, to the conservation of those metals and minerals of which the known supplies will be exhausted within a few decades. It is

well known that these are being 'wasted' now by being used for
purposes which could be as well served by regenerative materials;
by inadequate attention to reclamation and reconditioning for re-
use; and by unnecessary obsolescence. The 'waste' derives from the
fact that current market mechanisms attach no value as yet to the
prospective scarcity of these materials. In time, of course, scarcity
will make itself felt both as rising price and as constraint; and this
will no doubt be anticipated by political action both by supplying
and by fabricating countries. Those which live by fabricating cannot
afford to wait until constraint and rising prices signal the approaching end of a valued resource. The need for stability requires them to
look ahead, if need be to adjust both use and price and perhaps to
encourage search for alternatives by other means also. Each of the
main metals and minerals on which we now depend presents a
separate problem, to be examined in detail in its own right.

A study made by Sir Harold Hartley[2] in 1937 showed that at
that time about seventy-five per cent by value of the world's raw
materials were consumed as food. The fossil fuels accounted for
another ten per cent. Of the remaining fifteen per cent which formed
the 'raw materials' of all industries except food processing, one third
or more were natural products. Metals and minerals used in industry
were less than ten per cent of the whole and were at that time a
slightly decreasing proportion. This crucial ten per cent included
that smaller fraction which alone provides the materials for tools
and machines.

It would be useful to bring up to date the figures in Sir Harold
Hartley's analysis and to compare today's figures both in proportion
and in amount with those of 1937.

What different classes of use and in what proportions do the more
important metals and minerals now serve? Which of them are both
most important and least easily substituted by any technology now
in sight; and how rapidly are these demands growing? How far
could current rates of consumption be checked, without checking
overall production, by better conservation and recycling, substitution by natural products and reduced obsolescence? Tentative
answers even in the broadest terms would focus attention on problems which are neither tractable nor even visible when impending
shortages are looked at as a single threat.

Governments have and use now a battery of techniques for
affecting user both directly by imposing legal constraint and indirectly by modifying price. They use these techniques now in the
interests of stability—to anticipate and thus cushion the impact of
actual scarcity and constraint—no less than as instruments of other
policies. They will surely need to do so to a greater degree. Their

limitations will be largely set by the enlightenment of their citizens who will have to pay, in present cost and constraint, the price of mitigating much worse cost and constraint in the future. To answer such questions as these would be a first step in that enlightenment. I see no reason why these answers, however unpalatable, should be highly controversial.

Stability of Energy Supply

Everything already said about metals and minerals applies equally to the fossil fuels, except for two major and one minor qualification. Atomic fission offers an abundant energy supply over a long period, except in so far as it is limited by the radioactive pollutants which it produces. The extent of this limitation is hard to assess and harder to face when assessed and generates fierce argument among experts. But no one can regard as unimportant these growing radioactive graveyards. Nuclear energy by fusion, limited by little pollution except waste heat, is not yet invented; and if and when invented, it may be limited in use to countries capable of handling very high technology. So the question whether we can rely on nuclear energy for expanding energy supply in the future depends on a satisfactory answer to one or both of these queries. Neither has been answered yet to the sufficient satisfaction of the scientific or the lay community.

At a second remove comes the question whether other methods can be expected to produce massive energy directly from the sun. Photo-electric cells play an essential part on spacecraft but do not produce energy of a volume capable of doing massive work, as distinct from sending signals. Other methods are in the air, but not yet on the drawing boards. And the problem of storing energy without prohibitive weight remains unsolved. The policy makers of today should not make assumptions about the scientific achievements of the future until these have reached a stage where their viability is attested by the nearly universal assurance of the informed and especially the informed who are also independent. This applies also to the possibilities and limitations of synthesising fuels from materials more abundant than fossil fuels.

Finally there remain two inexhaustible sources of energy which may be globally unimportant but which might well be critical to some economies. These are the winds and the tides. The possibilities of a Severn barrage have often been debated but always rejected on economic, not technological grounds by comparison with fossil fuels. But the price of all the fossil fuels and their relation with each other and with atomic fuels is determined even now by political factors. These might change. They certainly would change if governments ceased to be able to count on abundant fossil or atomic fuels.

Thus the threat of a shortage of energy is less certain than the threat of a shortage of materials; but for that very reason it raises questions which are more important, as well as more difficult, to answer, yet which critically affect policy and action now. The British Government's present energy policy is based on assumed answers to these questions. The main questions in this sector which need to be answered are the limitations on atomically generated energy, by fission and by fusion, and the assumptions that can be made now about supplies from any of the alternative sources. These answers need to take into account physical constraints as well as cost. And in calculating cost they need to distinguish those elements which are artifacts of policy from those (if there are any) which reflect 'market' forces. Britain's atomic energy programme has suffered from the beginning from the fact that it was originally a by-product of a 'defence' demand for plutonium. And the British coal industry has recently shown that its future would be a political and social issue, even if Britain were not blessed with large supplies of a fuel which on present knowledge will far outlast all other fossil fuels.

By far the biggest unanswered question at this moment is the question whether we can or cannot assume that we shall in future command an unlimited non-polluting supply of energy, apart from that derived by biosynthesis. A world with abundant energy would be far more conscious of a shortage of metals but better able to mitigate the shortage, since synthetic materials usually consume in their production a great deal of power. But a world short of *either* metals and minerals *or* power, still more a world short of both, would be a world changed politically and ideologically, far more than technologically. It would be a world concentrated as never before on co-operating with the primary productive process, dependent and knowing its dependence on understanding both the limitations and the possibilities of that system.

The Limitations of Biosynthesis

The possibilities of this system may be capable of enormous expansion. Half the world is sea but sea farming has barely begun, though sea mining in some places may already have gone too far. The solar energy falling on the Sahara contributes scarcely at all to the organic explosion. The Amazon basin, large as Europe and receiving a sixth of the planet's rainfall, is a biochemical factory that

C

stuns the imagination. Yet it supports very poorly only 100,000 Amazonian Indians.

But the system also has its limitations, almost equally uncharted. The seas and lakes may be polluted before they can be farmed; and a major source of water pollution is the nitrogenous fertilisers now used in farming the land. Long-term artificial irrigation has its self-defeating trends. The Amazonian wilderness is the world's largest oxygen factory; whilst its soil, when cleared, has proved useless for agriculture and will not even revert to jungle.

With its possibilities and its limitations, this natural productive system must focus the attention of post-industrial man, as it focused the attention of agricultural man. But there will be two major differences. On the one hand, post-industrial man knows more both of the limitations and of the possibilities. On the other hand, he will progressively lack palliatives and easements that his agricultural ancestor could take for granted. Once there was unoccupied land to be developed, accumulated fertility to be enjoyed, primaeval forests to be used where they were not merely destroyed. Even his ignorance of farming kept in store for his future the possibilities of greater returns.

All these palliatives his post-industrial descendant must do without, including even the last. There is no reason to suppose that the productivity of the natural process can be increased without limit. We are far more aware today of fields where the limit has been passed, than of areas where it is still out of sight. And the more we look to the natural process for our materials and our processing as well as for our food, the more we shall press on its limits and the more we shall depend on restraining ourselves from over-passing them.

Pollution

Pollution also is a partly independent problem. Although it threatens to limit both industrial processes and farming it is also a threat in its own right to health, amenity and the quality of life.

Technologically, it may be a more manageable threat. Although there may be forms of pollution inseparable from populations of the number and density that will surely cover the earth over the next five decades (unless they are thinned by war, famine and pestilence) there is no other threat of pollution, present or anticipated, so far as I know, which could not be abated now—if the techniques of abating it can be made *politically* feasible and the costs *politically* tolerable. These are the limitations which technologists are prone to ignore. Abating pollution often means abating the activity which causes it or doing additional work to neutralise its effects. The political machinery is available; the political techniques are familiar. But once again the cure will impose on industry and agriculture additional costs and additional constraints. The technologist will be busier than ever. But far more work will have to be done to produce the same end product.

We can point to some achievements. The air of many cities is much less lethal than it was. Fish begin again to swim up English rivers that they have long avoided. On the other hand, as I write this, the British parliament, alerted by a recent scandal, is rushing through legislation to make it for the first time an offence to dump tons of poison on a rubbish dump.

Like the two fields already examined, pollution as such is too wide a category to be useful. It can be analysed either by reference to the kind of pollution caused, air, water, soil and so on, or to the polluting source. The first is needed in order to assess effects and trace polluting sources. The second is needed to distinguish the places where control has to be applied. Even a very summary analysis from both approaches would be useful to show the relative importance of varying kinds of pollution and the varying costs and benefits of dealing with them, calculated, of course, in terms of all relevant costs and benefits, rather than mere market calculations.

To consider, for example, the generation and disposal of solid waste—it is not *necessary* that solid waste, generated almost wholly by the private sector, should be disposed of almost wholly at the cost of the public sector. It is not *necessary* that the private generation of waste thus subsidised should be furthered by modern packaging methods, whilst the public sector should be debarred by 'expense' from using similarly modern methods of disposal.

The control of industrial by-products is more easily effected because the principle that the polluter should pay is more widely accepted and easier to apply. The most important enquiry in this direction would probably be to identify processes which cannot control their waste, have no prospect of doing so and are too important or too strongly entrenched to be easily scrapped. The present nuclear reactors are the obvious example. Almost equally serious are the agricultural problems discussed later.

More difficult perhaps are those pollutions which everyone knows will have to be controlled but which might be controlled in more than one, not necessarily consistent, way. The polluting power of the motor car could be reduced almost overnight by excluding lead from petrol. It could be reduced with rather greater delay by requirements for better combustion. It could be reduced in cities by substituting vehicles electrically powered. All these changes would have different costs and benefits and would operate on different time scales. But none of them would reduce the number of motor vehicles, so none of them would remove the 'pollution' of vehicular over-crowding with all its implications. Consequently, none of them would relieve the need to decide whether any, and if so, which parts of which cities shall replace private transport with public transport.

Probably the most difficult area of debate on pollution (embroiling both ideological and economic interests of great intensity) is the area of agricultural pollution. For several millennia agricultural man has been learning, through hideous errors, to expand without breaching the limitations of the natural productive process. The concepts of factory production, whether applied to agriculture or to animal husbandry, have raised production, encountered diminishing returns, produced some resounding disasters and generated mounting and well-earned distrust. Technologists and their paymasters, not only industry but equally the functional departments of government, are by-words for what may be called the instrumental approach—the choice of paths to a single goal simplified by excluding all costs and benefits except the benefit embodied in the goal and the immediate costs of attaining it as felt by the paymaster alone. This kind of objective—governed management—is the precise opposite of responsible regulation, which consists in managing through time a number of disparate, continuing relations; so there is every reason why not only ecologists but everyone with a sense of what government means should look askance at operators who are neither attuned by training nor compelled by the scope of their responsibility to consider all the benefits and count all the costs.

None the less, men on earth from now on will be increasingly concerned to improve the yield of the natural productive process and to do so without transgressing its limitations and so destroying the conditions on which it depends. This is the most fundamental of all exercises in preserving steady state—a state which needs to be no less steady whether production be rising or constant or declining.

Stability of Populations

The problems created by increasing populations are even more independent of the other sets of problems already discussed. They are social and political problems which would be overwhelming even if increasing economic growth were sufficient to meet the needs of the increasing billions. The combined restrictions of the other four factors will surely accentuate these problems by curtailing supplies and making even more difficult all policy decisions directed to holding the planetary state even a little more stable than brute fact will make it. For every move in the direction of control involves some abstinence today for the sake of a less disastrous tomorrow; and the more acute the present distress, the harder it will be for such measures to win acceptance. Hence much controversy centres on whether there is yet any real need for such sacrifices.

Such sacrifices would be needed now even if the future had no aggravating trends. As I have already argued, we need now, and shall continue increasingly to need, to shift an increasing proportion —not merely amount—of GNP to creating and maintaining a viable physical and social environment and to the increased investment per multiplying man that is an accompaniment of economic growth as now sustained, so long as this continues. It follows that even on present showing, the total available for personal consumption must decrease indefinitely unless the competing claims of collective use are to be denied until they explode; and the burden of this decrease is bound to fall on the upper half of the income pyramid. All the other trends noted in this chapter will accelerate this change but it is bound to occur even without them. The social and political implications are obvious.

Here also there is need and occasion to collect and publicise information, much of it uncontroversial. It is now almost universally agreed that populations will have to be stabilised, either by war, famine and pestilence or by human policy. Few would assume that *any* human policy must be worse than none; so the need for population policy is established, even if its possible scope is still uncertain. Any population policy needs to have some idea of optimum numbers or at least of tolerable maximum and minimum numbers for a given area. We need to know roughly what these would be on different assumptions. Important but simple studies need also to be made to show the differing effects of different kinds of change in population increase or decrease on population structure. Not all falling rates are due to falling *birth* rates; but those that are so caused reduce first the proportion of children and next the proportion of those of working age. Rapid changes in the rate will add their own problems of this kind.

But the major problems, as already observed, are political and social and will be in some ways worse if current rates of expansion are *not* curtailed. Mass democracy based on the universal franchise of a largely urban population is a relatively new device. Its major novelty is newer still; this is extreme *inequality* of wealth generated by *equality* of opportunity and unsupported by any other traditional support. It was not devised to control large populations for whom stability has become a paramount need, but for the precisely opposite condition, where growth was or seemed far more important than equitable distribution. These problems have to be faced in any case. It is important that they should not be presented as flowing from the other three problem areas and responding to the treatment of these areas. It seems to me much more likely that unsolved problems in the other areas will be needed to teach the multiplying populations to accept disciplines of membership which their own numbers would have made necessary in any event.

Some Pointers to Action Now

This summary of the familiar 'doomsday' theme seems to me to show that it invites analysis into five partially independent fields and about a dozen major problem areas. Each of these, I have suggested, can be explored at a level precise enough to guide policy and yet profound enough to be relevant to the total situation. Each can be explored factually rather than to provide arguments for an already determined policy, though some of them point so conclusively to unwelcome needs that they are bound to generate some of the controversy which should properly attend policy making rather than the appreciation of situations. This work urgently needs to be done. It is crucial that it be done at the right level. Too narrow a focus misses the major issues; too wide a focus misses their relative independence.

More controversially, I believe that these studies should be made *nationally*. The problems are indeed world problems and world action will have to be sought on many fronts. But the problems will fall unequally on every country—on countries with different climates and physical attributes; on countries developed and undeveloped in different degrees and for different reasons; and on countries over- and under-populated in different degrees, a spectrum unrelated to the degree of development. Moreover, national governments are the largest regulative authorities with even theoretic power to do what needs to be done. It is on them that the demands generated by these problems will fall. The demands on each will be different in character and in urgency. Each will be limited by its own degree of political competence. None will be able to defer its more urgent responses until agreement has been reached with others perhaps less closely involved, perhaps less capable of the necessary action. There will be a premium on action which each can take for itself. Moreover by exploring impending challenges to itself, each will be led early to distinguish those areas where useful action can only be taken in collaboration with others. It will thus be led to begin negotiations with these others earlier than it would otherwise have done. This will mitigate to some extent the danger that action taken by each to protect itself will hasten general disaster.

In Britain, for example, it is important to consider not only the world picture but also the particular strengths and weaknesses of this island, political, economic, geophysical and cultural. We are among the two or three most densely populated countries of the world; well watered but short of sunlight; fertile but dependent on others for half our food; rich in coal but short of metals; surrounded by tidal waters; heir to a long political and cultural tradition. The list of variables could be expanded indefinitely and it would be useful to consider which most deserve to be included in a manageably short list.

One other task demands to be done, more philosophic but not less practical. It is to relate our present ideas of linear, indefinite economic expansion to what needs to be our future idea of a stable though not necessarily static state. The natural productive process may be capable of much further development without impairing its stability. In many ways a more stable state would be a more human state and a more acceptable state, as well as a more governable state.

But our basic assumptions would be changed. Economists and technologists have regarded human industry as a process of converting materials which were drawn from an inexhaustible source and discarded into a bottomless sink. In such a world, cost is the expense to the maker of acquiring the material he needs and converting it into the products that he wants. There is no need for him to distinguish between products which can be naturally regenerated and those which cannot.

All these assumptions are failing. The source is dual and neither half is inexhaustible. Materials not naturally regenerated are irreplaceable and not necessarily open to substitution. Some of them will come to be regarded as a stock to be reclaimed and re-used; as we are already coming to regard our water supply. The true cost of using such resources includes the cost of recovering and reinstating them, so that they can be used again. This sharply distinguishes them from naturally regenerated products. These are subject to a different limitation. They are limited by the maximum rate to which the natural productive process can be speeded without damage to the conditions on which it depends. Nor is the sink bottomless. On the contrary it will become progressively more important to restrict what is thrown into it. To establish this view will have effects more far reaching than can be easily foreseen.

Whatever the results of these enquiries, they are bound to forecast important systemic changes which will impose increasing limitation on expansion in nearly all dimensions. It does not follow that they will impose, still less that they will lead men to design, a state which will be politically or socially 'steadier'. They will set the stage on which the human problems already defined, economic, political and social, will have to be solved—or not solved. Whether they make that task harder or easier depends largely on how well they are understood. Events on such a scale are not easily appreciated even when they are happening. To respond to them aptly in advance is infinitely harder. This, none the less, is a main object of education. And although formal education is, I believe, generally overrated as an agent of change, it deserves to be considered and its place assessed.

The Relevance of Present Instability

Whether limitation arises in relation to metals and minerals, fuels, pollution, biosynthesis or mounting populations, costs will be involved either in overcoming it or in adapting to it. These costs will be paid by someone, either in money or in deprivation, which will range from loss of amenity, through varying kinds and degrees of suffering, to death. These costs may to some diminishing extent be left to posterity, as most of them are now. In so far as they are not left to posterity, they will fall unequally on different societies, and within each society, and their distribution will be affected by policy, which will in turn be affected by changes in what people expect of the system, of each other and of themselves.

One general characteristic of these changes in distribution, as I have argued, must be a further shift of resources from individual to collective use. The need to monitor and maintain, if not to improve, the physical and social environment seems bound to claim a larger share even of smaller resources. A corresponding shift is likely to be needed from consumption to investment. If these needs are met, the costs—like the costs of not meeting them—will have to be met by individuals. In so far as they can be expressed in money, they will have to be paid by producers or consumers or tax payers.

It is useful to reflect on the political and social implications of these changes, even without any precise technological forecasting. But it is not useful or even possible to reflect on them without a realistic appreciation of the present trends on which they will impinge. For the main present problems of Britain and probably of other developed Western states are not problems of production or even, yet, of ecological imbalance. They are already now problems of distribution. I will briefly point to four areas of acute current instability which need to be better understood than they commonly are before

we can estimate the effect on them of an even mild trend towards a
steadier state.

(a) Inflation and Unemployment

Although the cost of living is rising at a dangerous rate, consumers
are being hugely subsidised by taxpayers as well as by posterity. It
would be useful to have even a rough estimate of the extent of this
subsidy and its sources. But whatever the figure, the difficulty of
removing the subsidy would be formidable, since if approached by
our present methods it would hugely increase the cost of living and
alter the real values of those personal incomes which focus most of
our conflicts and discontents, as well as affecting the balance of
payments.

This is largely due to an oddity of our present economic system
which would amaze a nineteenth-century economist. Vastly increased
productivity does not cheapen the product. It is more than wholly
absorbed in raising the rewards of those who use the productive
machines and in preparing to replace these by machines even more
productive and even more expensive. Employees claim to enjoy in
increased pay *at least the whole* of the increased profit produced by
the machines which they use but neither invent nor pay for; and they
claim it today as an ethical right. Looked at with eyes not dazed by
familiarity, it is an astounding claim and even more so when made
on grounds of equity rather than power. Can one conceive a primitive
tribe in which the hunters claimed to monopolise the increased bag
won with an improved bow? Our society is not less interdependent
but its distributive ethic is absurd.

From its absurdity two lethal consequences unfold. First, the
constantly over-priced producers compete ever less successfully with
the machines to which they owe their inflated earnings and speed
the vicious circle by which machines replace more of them and
further over-price the remainder. Secondly, their rewards set an
ethical level which powers the claim of those whose work, usually more
arduous and more skilled, cannot be multiplied by machines. These
claims partly conceded have the same effects to an even greater
degree in the labour-intensive industries and services but can never
meet the ethical criterion. Rising inflation, rising unemployment
and rising discontent are necessary results of such a system.

In a society so arranged that increased productivity went to reduce
prices, instead of raising the wages and salaries of the producers
directly concerned, producers would benefit *as consumers* by the increase in value of their unchanged earnings, which is precisely as
large a benefit as they deserve. The net increase in productivity would

appear as a fact after the event and would be distributed according
to consumption instead of being guessed in advance (always exaggerated) and distributed in advance to those who, it is hoped, will
produce it.

In so far as rises in productivity are not passed on in reduced cost,
we are driven to the familiar alternative of redistributing earnings
in the interest of more equitable incomes, having recovered them
from the recipients by direct taxation. This alternative is valuable
and indispensable. It is capable of much greater extension through
either or both of two principles.

One is to provide either by negative income tax or by some form
of 'social dividend' a supplement to all incomes below an acceptable
level. Professor J. E. Meade[3] has lucidly described how and why the
social security legislation based on the Beveridge report has fallen
so far short of its objective that the supplementary benefit scheme,
which in its original form was expected to catch only the occasional
unfortunate, has become the main agency in the reduction of poverty
in Britain, overworked and necessarily unsuccessful because of the
failure of other parts of the scheme to measure up to expectations.
I have no doubt that in one way or another the number of those
below the 'poverty line' will be reduced. Negative income tax, as
Dr Meade points out, has practical disadvantages. It has the
ideological advantage of expressing clearly and flexibly the current
policy for relating incomes to earnings. Any of these schemes if used
boldly enough would do something to mitigate the disparity of
reward between employment in capital-intensive and labour-
intensive industry. None of them is likely, in my view, to achieve
even its primary objective for long, so long as the 'poverty line' itself
continues to escalate under the pressures I have already described.

To divide workers into two classes separated by a subjective and
escalating divide may be necessary in present conditions and will, I
expect, always be necessary to take care of poverty not arising from
avoidable unemployment or under-paid employment. But no such
measure will of itself arrest the system's present built-in drive towards
inflation, towards unemployment and towards ever grosser disparity
of reward for human effort and skill, relative to machine minding.

These problems are with us now and would be urgent now even
if the promise or threat of 'steadier state' were a total illusion. It is
one aspect of the grossly unstable situation on which the demands of
'steadier state' will impinge. One effect, I hope, will be to dissipate
the illusion, cherished by socialists and non-socialists alike, that
growth can be relied on to correct inequities of distribution. This
will be welcome. Producers, as well as consumers and taxpayers, have
got to help pay the price of curing both unemployment and in-

flation. And the impact will fall not only on a rich or propertied or official minority but on everyone above today's average income. This would be true, even if the predictions of steadier state were a total illusion. It may well be, then, that the impact of 'steadier state' will be not so much to increase our present difficulties as to generate the will and point the way to their solution.

(b)   International Differentials and the Balance of Payments

Another already unstable area which will be notably affected for good and ill is the area of international relations. It is well accepted now that under the present system of international distribution, the gap between rich and poor nations widens and will go on widening. Scarcity of metals and minerals or of power would increase the economic bargaining power and make more precious the potential autonomy of some under-developed and still lightly populated countries, especially those with still unused scope for extended biosynthesis. This would help to restore the complementary element in international trade which a century ago moved political economists to enthusiasm far more than their trust in competition. It would be useful to estimate how far and how soon trends towards steadier state might move the terms of trade in favour of major sources of raw materials. It seems to me unlikely, however, that present trends towards greater inequality will be thereby reversed. History has bequeathed to us the belief that international trade, like intra-national trade, can and should expand indefinitely and that this expansion can and should be *both* self-balancing *and* mutually enriching. And a further development of this mythology insists that these three trends should be sustainable without more than mild and occasional changes in exchange rates. These beliefs do not seem to me sustainable by any analysis of international exchange, either in real or in monetary terms. Any greater stability in international exchanges imposed either by policy or necessity is likely to reduce the volume of international trade. And we have as yet no adequate alternative means of redressing international disparities of income. Thus the problem of adjusting differences in earnings is even further from solution internationally than nationally. Yet internationally, no less than nationally, the value of competition as a regulator is declining as the area shrinks in which winners can afford to be indifferent to the plight of losers. The balance of payments is still regarded as a national problem. Yet it is at least as embarrassing for creditors as for debtors when debtors cannot pay their debts.

(c)   Political Instability

It seems evident that any trend towards steadier state will require more regulation, national and international, political, economic and social and will therefore increase the load on all our existing regulative machinery, especially the State. But this load is increasing *now* and political instability mounts *now* because the governed, in so many developed countries, are withdrawing their confidence in their governments' judgment of what needs to be done or its capacity to do what is needed or both. (Either or both may conceal their own unwillingness to pay the price which would fall on them personally.) Whatever the origin of this lack of confidence (which is justly reflected in governments' reciprocal mistrust of those they govern) it is with us *now*. The impact of 'steadier state', whilst making even more demands on it, may well generate, in governments and governed alike, the responses that now are lacking. It is hard to imagine a developed country supporting these impacts without amplifying public power to a level comparable with that attained by Britain in the latter stages of the Second World War. At that time government directed what almost everyone should do, rationed what anybody could enjoy, controlled the activities of all businesses and exercised total financial control. Yet it was a very human and in many ways a very unstressful world. Almost everyone could afford what they needed. No one, however rich, could get any more. The necessities of life were more equitably distributed and its burdens more commonly and willingly shared than perhaps at any time before or since. It was none the less a world of enormous political control. Those controls, I have no doubt, will be generated again, either by human foresight or by the disasters which the lack of human foresight will engender. But the instability which will provoke them will not be engendered by trends towards steadier state. The seeds are germinating now.

(d)   Education

It is no accident that our age should be beset by doubts about the relevance of its educational curricula. We need to understand our *current* situation; not merely the future that we are preparing for ourselves. If we did so, we would be equally fitted to understand or anticipate trends towards 'steadier state'. Not only in higher education but even more in secondary and primary education, not only in specialist but in general education, not only in the few but in the many, we need to develop an understanding of the way we are related to each other, our present to our future, our benefits to our costs. Education may not be in itself a potential social determinant but it is invaluable and irreplaceable in preparing us, old as well as young, to learn from each other and from experience. It urgently needs to be rethought now for the needs not merely of tomorrow but of today. I return to this need in Chapter 10.

This does not purport to be an exhaustive list of the areas in which we need to seek now for political and social implications of any trend towards a steadier state. In each of them we find that the key to the future lies in understanding the present. This reinforces the argument that we need not wait until the technological forecasters have finished arguing. The more crucial issues can be decided on information which should be available now. And in so far as they cannot be so decided, they will indicate what questions the technological forecasters are most urgently required to answer and with what degree of precision. This may help both to shorten and to focus an argument, of which the only valuable products can be human policies and human expectations more enlightened, more rational and more humane than they are now.[4]

Notes and References

1. The factors here distinguished differ slightly from those used by Professors Forrester and Meadows. It seems to me useful, at least for the present, to distinguish between fossil fuels and other unregenerative resources and also between food and other products of biosynthesis.
2. Sir Harold Hartley, F.R.S. 1937. The Mather Lecture. *Journal of the Textile Institute.* XXIII. No. 7.
3. J. E. Meade. Poverty in the Welfare State. *Oxford Economic Papers.* Vol. 24, No. 3, Nov. 1972, pp. 289–326.
4. This chapter first appeared in *Futures,* December 1972.

PART II

Institutions and Persons

CHAPTER 5

The End of the Individualist

The Making of the Individualist

In the year 1540 a play called *The Three Estates* was performed in a castle in Scotland. It was written by a courtier and played before a king, but it was as radical as a Civil Rights manifesto.

When I saw it 400 years later, the characters representing the three estates were grouped round three sides of a great square stage. On one side was the civil power, with its governors and judges. On another was the Church, with its prelates and its pardoners. On the third side was the power of property, represented by the burgesses. Along the fourth side of the stage surged the common people, the fourth estate, with their spokesman, a splendid character called John the Commonweal, who accused the three corrupt, oppressive powers in gloriously uninhibited language and humbled them all before an august figure called Divine Correction.

John symbolises one element in our many-sided concept of the individual. He is a human being, with rights and feelings, like each of us; and he has the courage to stand up for himself and his fellows against the strong, in the name of justice and conscience. The theme was old in 1540 but the note in John's voice was new. Before that time, this was not at all the kind of play that a courtier would write to entertain a king.

John is a symbol still very much alive, especially in the United States, to which so many Johns have come from other lands to escape the oppression of the Church or the State or the rich. For centuries they came largely from Britain. After their descendants had hailed poor George III before Divine Correction and set up their own power structure, they were joined by Johns from many other lands, who shared their faith in the individual or learned it from them.

Since 1540, four centuries of history have woven other elements into our picture of the individual; they are doing so today more actively than ever before. We need to distinguish them, for they are not easy to reconcile.

In the hard centuries before the affluent society emerged, immigrant John was challenged not by Church or State or property but by nature. His human relations were beautifully simplified. He was bound to a small group of neighbours by specific mutual needs for help in tasks where each needed the joint strength of all—in defence and the keeping of public order and a few major tasks on the land. For the rest, he and his family lived by their own strength and skill. John the individual became for the first time an individualist.

His astonishing success set him the problem of identity with which he is wrestling now. A largely urban money economy has reversed his relations both with his fellows and with the physical world. Faceless crowds surround him, instead of scattered neighbours; and he is consciously bound to them, if at all, by mere propinquity, occasionally by affection, sometimes by fear but scarcely ever by apparent mutual need. Yet these same neighbours exercise far more power over him and he over them by almost everything they do. He cannot move without restricting the freedom of movement of those around him or live without adding to the pollution of their common air; and he must suffer the same from them in countless ways and in increasing measure.

It is a frustrating position for an individualist.

Time and success have equally reversed his relation with the physical world. For John the immigrant, physical nature was the dominant fact of life. Indifferent to him, it yet sustained or starved him, destroyed him or made him rich. It was resource, partner, enemy and friend. Today, for the great majority of his descendants, it has eerily disappeared behind an institutional system, which spews from one spout a huge abundance of natural and unnatural products and sprays from another spout the tokens with which to buy them. This elusive, ubiquitous System has taken the place of field and forest as his basic environment.

The System has another aspect, almost equally faceless; immense, collective political power. Each individual within it depends increasingly on this collective power for those necessities of life which until yesterday were either free or for him to make for himself. Air, sanitation, water, transport, living space, working space; education and information; all that makes life viable for him is provided and can only be provided for him by massive organisation, over which he has and can have little control. Tomorrow the whole urban environment will be viable only in so far as it is not an aggregate but an artifact, shaped with art and prescience for needs foreseen at least a decade ahead and itself potent to create the future that it foresees.

This crowded, urbanised world will call for qualities in its individual citizens different from those they needed in more individualist days; for more patience and tolerance; more intelligence, to understand far more complex situations; a far more distant time horizon; a wider sense of responsibility; more sensitivity to people; less of that aggressive maleness on which individualists (assumed to be male) so prided themselves and less of the qualities that go with it (and why not, seeing that half the world are women?). It will curtail many opportunities that individualists valued and bring many new ones that individuals may value more. None of these changes are in themselves threats to 'The Individual'. On the contrary, they make room for individuals of far greater variety and require of them all higher intelligence, more capacity for human relations and greater self-control and offer them all wider opportunities for significant human life.

They also bring threats—new, real and serious threats—to human individuality. These too we must consider. But let us not confuse threats to the outmoded concept of the individualist with threats to those far more essential conditions on which individuality depends.

The promises of the future are commonly conceived as the promises of technology—leisure, an abundance of buyable goods, huge resources for manipulating the physical world and (within still undefined limitations) even greater facilities for handling 'information'. Its responsibilities are those involved in managing and keeping human the world which such technology creates. Its threat is the looming possibility that this world may be incapable of nourishing the individuality or the enormously enhanced responsibility which will be needed to control it. More precisely, the threat is that technology will magnify man the doer and dwarf man the done-by; that it will escape from the economic and the political control of its users and its beneficiaries and establish a senseless, self-exciting cycle of activity in which both are enslaved; that it will make a world too large in size and too mixed and impoverished in culture to breed the responsibility needed to control it; and that, conceived in mechanistic terms, it will dehumanise its participants by a mechanistic ideology.

The Passing of the Individualist

If David Lindsay, the author of that old satire-cum-morality play, could return to earth and revise it for us today, the stage would still be ringed by at least four estates. The power of government, the power of orthodoxy and the power of money are still to be recognised and still to be feared. John has still cause to attack them and has still some generally accepted principles to which to appeal against them. He is making more threatening noises at them in twentieth-century America and Britain than he made in sixteenth-century Scotland.

But the play, and even the players, would be different. The Church would no longer represent the voice and power of trans-national authority. Its place would be taken by the scientific and technological establishment. A new estate would have appeared on the stage—organised labour, at least as powerful as any of the other three, and nearly as remote from the rest of the common people who used to form the fourth estate. And even they, now the fifth estate, would have to be accommodated on the stage, for they are no longer merely sufferers and protestors, but agents, possessing so much power, especially power to negate, that they can no longer criticise their governors without criticising themselves.

There would therefore be a much less self-righteous role for John the Commonweal, whether we think of him as trade union leader, upholder of civil rights or spokesman of the poor. He is as liable as any other party on the stage to be *called to account* as oppressive, even as merely irresponsible; and so is each member of the crowd he represents. The net of responsibility has become, logically if not yet in practice, far more reciprocal and far more universal.

It has also in some degree changed its character. Today whatever else may threaten, each is threatened by all; and not so much by the others' wickedness as by their collective impotence to control the system which their collective activities create. And in regulating this conflict, the principles to which appeal can be made are far less coherent and far less agreed. For the new threat derives in part from that very individualism which feels itself threatened. The next fifty years may or may not make a world more fit for individuals to live in but it will certainly not make a world more acceptable to individualists.

Many of those independent men and women who settled the American continent came there to escape the power structure of other lands; but their descendants have built for themselves a new power structure so vast as to dwarf every one of those old tyrannies. They have built it and they need it; they cannot live without it. And for each of them, his share in the control of this power structure grows ever less, whilst his dependence on it and his duties towards it grow ever greater.

Consider the future of the physical environment, a visible and relatively simple problem when compared with our other environments.

To keep our urban societies viable over the next fifty years will require very large-scale, long-term action, directed to designing, creating and maintaining the urban environment and containing the threats which its own activities engender, such as the pollution of air and water, the overload of transport and communications and mutually frustrating land uses. In this operation man the done-by will have to accept and support and help pay for these massive operations, even though he knows—or will soon discover—that they are planned in conditions of such doubt and risk that they will often prove to have been mis-conceived.

This will involve a major shift in priorities, in attitudes, in commitments, even in the ways in which we conceptualise our common situation. These new priorities, attitudes, commitments and concepts are at variance with those now widely held. The same individuals must participate actively in the debate which revises them.

These two requirements are hard to combine. Massive action needs the support of widespread confidence in its rightness; it marks the ages of faith. Rapid change in our priorities and commitments needs readiness to question the accepted, to explore the unwelcome, to tolerate the shocking. It marks the ages of doubt. Somehow we have to combine the attitudes of both. Can it be done? If so, how and at what cost? What does it imply?

It implies first, I think, the ability to tolerate greatly increased frustration, without lapsing into apathy or escapism or erupting into polarised conflict. This frustration is with us now in two forms. We have frustration at the slowness of change; decades intervene between the time when some bit of the urban environment is recognised as intolerable and the time when it is effectively re-made. Equally, we have frustration at the inability to prevent change, by those whom it threatens. The beneficiaries of the *status quo* are right to feel threatened by its erosion, just as its victims are right to feel threatened by its inertia. Yet both will have to tolerate far greater degrees of these threats.

The situation calls for more than toleration; it demands participation at several levels, each of which raises acute difficulties.

It requires some participation in planning and policy making at the local level. The physical redesign of our local world affects us intimately. The planned-for are already insisting on their rights to be consulted, with a vehemence which would command attention, even if planners were not aware of their need to secure emotional and intellectual support. Yet both conditions are beset with almost impassable barriers. Even where planning is on the same scale as the personal interests and awareness of the members of an existing community, the divergent interests of these members, on whom the costs and benefits are bound to fall capriciously, make agreement difficult; and the power of local vested interests is greatest at this level. Even more difficult is the situation, increasingly more common, where the scale of planning exceeds, both in space and time, that of any existing community today. In any case, the individuals who will most greatly suffer or benefit from any plan of adequate scale are unborn or in their cradles. They have no lobby; and their local progenitors are not necessarily best fitted to speak for them. The problem of participation at this level has not yet been solved or shown to be soluble.

This participation needs to be fortified by emotional involvement in the expected result. If the urban environment is to change fast enough to keep pace with our needs, most of us will be conscious most of the time of physical change going on around us, of its concomitant social change and of its inherent cost, inconvenience and, probably, threat. Can this be offset by real emotional and intellectual participation in the operation and its planned result? This was sometimes possible in past ages, when cities shone like beacons in the wilderness of 'nature' and symbolised both the achievements of the human spirit and its home. It remains to be seen whether our contemporary urban societies can recapture such an attitude on the scale of today.

A third and perhaps the most critical level of participation is in the adventure of reshaping our values and priorities, so as to make dominant the task of creating collectively the milieu on which the quality of our lives will increasingly depend. This intellectual adventure is not confined to intellectuals. Yet here, as in all pioneering of the human spirit, the vision comes first to few; and a minority must do the arduous and thankless task of advocating and displaying the new pattern, until it has been naturalised in the minds of the many. It involves that free but disciplined dialogue which lies at the heart of the democratic process. Dialogue on this scale has never yet been achieved.

These tasks are formidable; the conditions are exacting; and the limitations are rigid. The first of these limitations is time. Of the men and women who will sit in seats of power and influence—including negative influence—over the next fifty years, most are alive now. Nothing done to change the physical, intellectual and emotional milieu can alter that which it has already laid down in most of them, their basic possibilities and limitations in interpreting and responding to the future.

A further limitation is the rate of change to which the future will compel these individuals to respond as best they may. Some of these variables are at present beyond control or prediction. Such for example, is the rate of change in the numbers of the population and the course of racial and political stress both within the society and between it and others. Other variables, such as the effect of automation on employment, command as yet no agreement on their future course or on the extent to which they can or should be controlled. These changes occur in three main dimensions—in the physical pattern of life; in its institutional pattern; and in the conceptual pattern which represents it in our minds. Conceptual changes are often the slowest or, if speeded, the most disruptive of any. This quickening of the rate of change in all three dimensions is, I believe, a main cause of the malaise which afflicts us.

Another element is the growing disparity between the scale of cultural and social life on the one hand and of economic and political life on the other. Culturally, we want to live in a world of human scale; and we are learning both by experience and by scientific study how small such worlds must be, especially if they are to preserve continuity through change without impoverishment. Yet politically and economically, we seem to be committed to a system which can be hardly less than global.

Yet something more than all this, I think, is needed to explain the casualties which litter the social landscape. These are obvious and all too familiar—in one direction, rootlessness, anomie and alienation; in another, withdrawal and escapism; in another, predatory symbiosis; in another, fanatical dedication to an orthodoxy which forbids dissent or discussion; in yet another, the shallow anodyne of commercialised distraction. All these are signs of 'individuality' breaking down or preserving itself at prohibitive social cost. A culture which is to preserve individuality in a collective age must be more than a mixture of these dreary ingredients.

To define our most radical threat—and equally, our most radical hope—let us look back again at the age of *The Three Estates*.

The End of the Renaissance

The year 1540, in which *The Three Estates* was first produced, saw the first published account of Copernicus' new astronomy. Michelangelo and Martin Luther were living; Machiavelli and Leonardo da Vinci were a few years dead. It was the high Renaissance. Men were discovering and creating new forms and shattering old ones, in science, art, geography, politics and religion. Both the conceptual and the physical worlds were expanding dizzily. Social criticism was seething. Rival orthodoxies were feuding. It was an age, in these ways, very like our own.

But it was not an age of exploding technology. In 1540 the printing press was already nearly a century old, the telescope still nearly a century in the future. Techniques were moving; but their headlong rush had not begun. From this difference, I think, springs that feature of our age which would most shock Michelangelo.

This is the difference to which we are coming to attribute our distresses and our anxieties and I think we are right in doing so; but the effect of it is manifold and indirect and its most obvious aspect is not, I think, the most important.

The most obvious impact of technology is on the physical conditions of life and thus on the growth in numbers of human populations and in the escalation of their material expectations. The importance of this, as I have argued throughout this book, lies in the corresponding increase in the ethical demands which it makes on each of them, that is, in what it requires them to expect of each other and therefore of themselves.

But 'technology' became an agent of growth and change only when it became the instrument of an entrepreneurial system capable of using it on a large scale, geared to expanding it and dependent on its expansion for its own success. It was the marriage of technology to capitalism which made it fertile. It was not the marriage of technology and science. That was to come later. Only in our day when science itself has become big business, has the interaction of science and technology become in itself a potent agent of change. And even this combination is only a sub-system of the government-entrepreneurial system analysed in earlier chapters.

None the less, science and technology were potent agents of ideological change long before they began to transform the physical conditions of life. One of these changes I shall trace in later chapters. It is a basic change in the concept of order. For John the Commonweal the world was still divinely ordered. A century later the radical elements of Cromwell's New Model Army had already conceived it possible that men might order their own world and were questioning the existing order in a way which alarmed those who had made the revolution and armed them to fight it. Christopher Hill[1] has traced in fascinating detail the rise of this revolution within a revolution and the proliferation of its dreams. It failed but it was to recur, never more violently than today. And whenever it recurs, it poses the same challenge. By what standards shall a society order itself and legitimise the authority which sustains that order?

I believe that this question has an answer; but science and technology, though they posed the question, were to obscure the answer and hamper men in their search for it for three centuries. The natural scientist was an observer, discerning regularities in the natural world. The technologist was a manipulator, seeking means to ends. Neither attitude was adequate or apt to men who aspired to be architects of a human world which could only be built in the ethical dimension.

Hence sprang that feature of our age which would most have shocked Michelangelo—our preoccupation with non-human processes and non-human ways of thinking. No doubt his age was in many ways more harsh, less sensitive than ours; yet ours blights us in ways from which his age was free. It encloses us in a system of non-human scale; with this I have already briefly dealt. It focuses our attention on non-human objectives: how else could the richest country in the world spend half its government's revenue on weapon systems and space exploration? It constrains us to view men and their activities in non-human ways; how else could a writer on managerial efficiency voice orthodoxy when he writes—'Efficiency in operations results from arranging conditions of work in such a way that *human elements interfere to a minimum degree.*' What would Michelangelo have made of that?

We should not blame technology as such for this pernicious ideology; yet it has grown with the growth of technology and in close association with it. It springs in part from that preoccupation with material things which characterised the rise of the physical sciences. The huge success of their method depreciated all knowledge gained in other ways and therewith nearly all our important knowledge of human life. It debased the concept of reason, equating it with a logical process which could not explain even the activity of scientists in laboratories. It entered into partnership with a productive system which first depersonalised men to the level of productive units and is now depersonalising them still further to the level of mere consumers, supported on condition that they keep the automata at work.

The men of the Renaissance would have been amazed and appalled, if they could have divined that a movement powered by so great an urge to liberate the human spirit would shut it up in a prison of its own devising; that a world designed to the measure of man would be built to the measure of his machines. Yet this is what is happening and the lethal trend will not easily be reversed.

We are engaged on an adventure which has no successful precedent and no logical inference that I can draw assures its success or even makes success probable. It is seen most clearly when we consider what is involved today merely in the shaping of the urban environment.

For the obvious and compelling need to design and create our own physical environment focuses in the clearest way the human criteria which define success and places scientific knowledge and technological know-how in their proper perspective. Science begins to give us means to picture to ourselves the system within which we are acting. Technology enlarges our means of acting on it. But the choice of how to act remains the task of human judgment, nurtured in the emergent values of its age and crystallised by the need to re-shape those that most offend it.

I believe that aesthetic judgment is the ruling passion of truly human kind; and I deliberately call judgment a passion. By aesthetic judgment I mean the passionate but patient struggle to bring significant form into being whether what we have to shape is a city, an institution, a public policy or a personal life; knowing that what makes the new form significant is itself a product of time, that the standards by which it is judged will be changed even by being realised.

A Copernican revolution will be needed to restore this faculty to its place of honour. It will represent a system revolving round a centre more sophisticated than our present concept of the Gross National Product, which includes only what is bought and sold and compares these only by the values of the market place.

It is possible to hope that the making of the City will be a task sufficiently concrete, sufficiently comprehensible and yet sufficiently noble to bring together man the doer and man the done-by in a single on-going act of creation. For the City represents in concrete form the realisation of many human values. For good or ill, it expresses our sense of physical form, of functional fitness and functional priorities, of social justice and social compassion, of joy in nature and art, in companionship and even in solitude. It is a way of life, as well as a place to live; its inhabitants, as well as its planners, participate in its creation. Even when it has grown beyond the human scale, as it has in the great conurbations, it contains recognisable areas that challenge us in the name of all these values to make them anew. As the proliferating city at its worst is a symbol of dehumanisation today, so the created city might tomorrow be a symbol of life made again to the measure of man's potentialities.

The people of the United States cover half a continent and are numbered in hundreds of millions. They range in condition between extremes of endowment and disendowment, physical, emotional, intellectual and even economic. More than in most other countries, they are knit in a web of varying sub-cultures, reflecting differences not only local, educational, occupational and economic but also differences of origin; for more than one-seventh of them are children of parents born in other lands and more than another tenth, and these among the oldest families in the country, are of African descent. This rich variety cannot be reduced to one admired type, least of all, perhaps, to The Individualist.

Yet it remains essential that all these sub-cultures should have in common the kind of cultural seedbed in which individuality can grow. It is essential to the development of people and no less essential to their society; for all creative innovation comes from individual people. This seedbed is itself a social artifact and so is the climate in which such seeds can grow. John could voice no protest unless he had been taught common concepts and common norms and a common language in which to appeal to them; and he would be unlikely to protest and still less likely to be listened to, except in a society which had taught him and his neighbours to expect this of themselves and each other.

The question is whether a society so vast, so new, so mixed and so dynamic can contain such a dialogue within a coherent, corporate life. It is the problem of all Western societies, but, as usual, it is displayed in the United States more dramatically and on a grander scale. I believe that the task of building the City epitomises the problem in the form and on the scale most likely to release the creative and self-educative forces of a community and thus concentrates our concern on what is the most fruitful and the most hopeful, as well as the most urgent problem of our day.

[Based on a paper prepared for a conference on the Next Fifty Years organised by the American Institute of Planners in 1966 and published in William R. Ewald Jr. (Editor) *Environment and Change,* 1968, Indiana University Press.]

Reference

1. Christopher Hill. *The World Turned Upside Down.* 1972. London. Temple Smith.

CHAPTER 6

Us, Them and It

Loyalty and Alienation

Men have always depended on some group to which they were conscious of belonging and have looked out across its boundaries at other men to whom they were not so bound. This divide between those who call themselves 'us' and others who they regard as 'them' is a social reality of great importance.

Through nearly the whole of human existence one small group comprised virtually *all* the human relations of *all* its members—both the relations on which they actually depended and those on which they felt themselves to depend. In such conditions there is little or no divergence either between felt loyalties and actual dependence or between rival groupings making conflicting claims to loyalty.

Both these divergences have multiplied in the last few millennia and especially in the last few centuries. Nets of mutual dependence link men as members of families, neighbours, citizens, nationals and earth-dwellers; as members of business organisations and of unions formed to fight those organisations; as members of professions and scientific disciplines; as adherents of religions and ideologies and political parties; as members of racial communities. Each of these has both an objective and a subjective aspect. Some, intensely felt, are objectively weak. The adult members of most Western families, for example, usually depend on each other neither for protection nor for economic support. But they may none the less feel a strong sense of family solidarity and be psychologically supported thereby. Others, objectively strong, are ignored or intensely resented. Englishmen today for example depend on their membership of their political state to an extent undreamed of a hundred years ago. Yet the sentiment of patriotism is far weaker. Even intellectual recognition of their dependence is so deeply obscured that many of them are proud to deny it. I shall examine in a later chapter the nature and relation of these two aspects of human interdependence. I am concerned here to examine the results of this proliferation of claims to loyalty.

This is commonly welcomed as a safeguard against the polarisation of conflict between any group of 'us' and the residual, alien 'them'. And it is true that we need to be bound by a web of relationships, if none is to be all-embracing. But the more complex the web, the greater the demands it makes on the individual's power to resolve conflict. In consequence few of us are consciously ruled by a pattern of loyalties nearly so complex as that demanded by the pattern of systems on which we in fact depend.

The more comprehensive the bonds which link men to a given system, the more alien will appear all those who are external to it. And all groups and societies, mindful of their own coherence, do what they can to make their own claims dominant and to weaken any claims which might conflict with their own. Nation states in particular have focused, fomented and gloried in such all-embracing loyalties and their claims cannot abate so long as their members' claims on them and theirs on their members grow ever more comprehensive.

Where the felt and the real dependence of membership in a single system is extensive, whilst cross links with those outside the system are weak, the system's internal coherence will be strong but it will be prone to treat those outside as part of that environment to which no duty is felt to be due. Totalitarian states and some trade unions are familiar examples. When wider loyalties, both real and felt, *cut across* the system's boundaries, as international trade and international science cut across and qualify the boundaries of national systems, the system's autonomy will be curtailed, probably both for good and for ill. When wider loyalties both real and felt, comprehend the system with other systems, a different form of conflict ensues. It usually results in integrating the smaller with the larger system in some degree but often at the cost of weaker coherence, less initiative and more sluggish response. These fears have been conspicuous in the debate in Britain about joining the European Economic Community.

There is, however, another type of change, particularly relevant to our present situation, when the felt, even though not the real, bonds within a system are loosened, without being replaced by the rival claims of another system. This is the situation which I examined in Chapter 1 where society is threatened not by conflicts of loyalty but by simple evaporation of loyalty. The felt claims of membership become inadequate to support the real interdependence from which that membership arises. A gulf widens—the widening gulf discussed in Chapter 1—between the individual and *all* the large-scale systems on which he depends and to which he is consequently required to respond.

In earlier chapters I have traced some of the steps by which membership and especially membership of a political society, once the accepted base of individual life, more recently eclipsed, has again become dominant. In this chapter I will pursue the causes and the implications of this a little further.

So long as government and its associated class structure were regarded as part of a divine or natural order, criticism focused not on its institutions but on the people who sat in their seats of power. Men had standards by which to judge their officials; they knew what they meant by a good king or a just judge and they had no doubt that these were good things that they wanted. John the Commonweal, in the old play already mentioned, did not attack Church or State or property as such; only their corrupt representatives. The short-comings of individuals were seen as private vices and weaknesses, magnified but not justified by the opportunities which office gave for displaying them. Official roles were conceived as in themselves ennobling.

Moreover, official roles did not differ sharply in character from occupational and social roles. The farmer, the trader, the artisan, like the noblemen, the employer, the neighbour, were roles which could be judged well or ill played by standards which were sufficiently well accepted. Every role was social. From Homeric times to a date not so very far astern, the quality of a man was largely judged both by his fellows and by himself by comparing his performance in all his social roles with contemporary standards of what was 'good'. The distinction between public and private roles was muted or even absent.

A major change came over this scene when men ceased to regard the 'order' which distributed wealth, power and function as divinely appointed or even defined by 'nature' and came instead to regard it as an arrangement devised and imposed by men on men, which men could alter to accord with their ideas of justice or convenience.

Once institutions lost their 'established' status, they became the focus both of intense hostility and of extravagant hope. As human artifacts, they became legitimate objects of criticism by all those who felt ill served by them or thought their activities unjust or inefficient or misdirected. Although the flood of criticism thus released has worked much good, it has eroded the authority of all established institutions and thus reduced their power to resolve or contain conflict, which is their main social function.

It has also eroded the status of their office holders. The critic of an institution cannot afford to allow that its badness may be even partly due to the performance of its office holders or that better official role playing might redeem it. The quality of the official tends to be seen as a function of the design and purpose of the institution and especially of the means by which officials are held to account and the standards by which they are judged.

These effects were to be fully felt only after the initial hopes in institutions had abated.

The Institutional Environment

These hopes were three-fold. First there was hope of establishing control over political institutions, making them responsible to those whom they served. The more ancient form of this hope went no further than the aspiration to choose governors and to control what they did, partly by making laws to which they would be no less subject than others and partly by controlling their revenues. The French Revolution introduced a more ambitious concept. This identified representative government with self-government to an extent unlikely to be realised by any society which is not more coherent and like-minded than most societies would wish to be. An English writer on political theory in a book already mentioned has called this 'the heresy of democracy'.[1] It contributed to the extravagant hopes which were born at that time. And by opening up the whole field of institution building to the energy and ingenuity of men, it raised two further and significantly different hopes for the future of institutions. Brought under the control of the common man, and so no longer a threat, institutions could be of infinite service to him in producing the goods and services and political regulations that he wanted. And further, in so far as he was a creature of his environment, they could remake him and his environment together. Social engineering, as well as social service, was implicit in the new promise. Hopes of universal education spanned the two.

The 19th century in England has been called the century of hope. Some of these hopes centred on the individual, some on his institutions. Both had limits and inherent inconsistencies which were barely visible then but which are all too obvious now. All were based on the assumption that the individual, as consumer of both political and economic services, could and would determine what they should be, to his own and his neighbour's satisfaction. This is the doctrine that Professor Galbraith has called consumer dominance.[2] In both the political and the economic dimension it has disappointed what were extravagant hopes.

The political disappointment is well known. For a century lovers of freedom and equality marched to the left, singing songs before sunrise. But the cold and eerie light which illumines the close of our century does not look like the rising sun. One-party governments have not realised the hopes which brought them to power. Two-party and multi-party governments are widely denounced as unresponsive, as well as incompetent. This is partly because so many articulate but discordant voices are now free to call on them for incompatible responses. It is equally due to the fact that responsible governments need responsible people, and are impotent when these are lacking. The British people, as I write this (1971), are in the inglorious position of having refused to both their alternative governments the power to regulate that inflation which most distresses them.

But before pursuing the disappointed hopes in political institutions we need to follow the breakdown of consumer dominance on the economic side.

Suppliers in a classical market were all subordinate to the wishes of the consumer. This mythical character, immune alike to envy and to advertising, knew just what he wanted and how to deploy his resources through the market so as best to satisfy his wants. Suppliers, none of whom were supposed to be large enough to influence the market, could only achieve success by meeting his preferences more cheaply and aptly than their competitors. No ethical choices were needed to keep producers in the service of consumers. The hidden hand turned universal self-seeking to the good of all.

The irony of Professor Galbraith has been persuading his economic colleagues, as laymen had been persuaded somewhat earlier, that this model no longer represents our world sufficiently to be useful. In The New Industrial State producers have power and use power according to their institutional criteria of success. The entrepreneurial system has largely escaped from the control of the individual who in any case had no means, even if he had the vision, to express through the market his preferences for those collective goods and services, such as roads and health and education, on which his well-being increasingly depends. Hence the growth of regulations and ethical aspirations which seek to restrain and direct the entrepreneurial system in the public interest.

The dethronement of the consumer as controller of organised production has also destroyed the theoretic limitation on the power of trade unions. So long as producers could satisfy employees only out of profits won in a free market, the pressure of organised labour could only improve employers' efficiency and distribute their profits more equitably. This world is even further in the past. Wage negotiations today, national in scope, have indeed multiple effects; they largely determine prices and the wage differentials of competitive groups of workers as against each other and collectively as against the unorganised. They affect the level of business investment, the rate of inflation and the balance of payments. But they have little effect on company profits; and they raise rather than lower the incomes of those who now sit in the seats of the bosses.

Thus both industry and trade unions have largely passed out of that automatic control which was once predicated on consumer dominance. Yet it was only through reliance on this that they were allowed to come into existence. These dominant realities of our culture, the limited company and the trade union, are barely a century old. Until the mid-19th century the right to form a corporation, especially one which could earn and accumulate profits indefinitely, was a jealously guarded privilege, exercised only by Royal charter or special act of parliament. Trade unions were legitimised even later. Both these djinns were let out of their bottles because our grandfathers believed that market mechanisms could control them. We know now that they cannot.

As faith waned in an automatically self-regulating system, so political regulators were increasingly called in to redress the balance. Even in the 19th century they were used to regulate hours and conditions of labour. Today their scope includes employment, credit, the balance of payments and the gigantic redistribution of incomes described in the previous chapters. But in the course of this development the institutions of government, business and labour have become enmeshed in the mutually dependent but self-exciting and thus unstable system already mentioned, which limits the initiatives of political decision. I have described this system elsewhere more fully than space here permits.[3] Briefly, the entrepreneurial system depends on the government system not only to assure all its basic conditions but also as its chief customer, whilst the governmental system depends on the entrepreneurial system, directly and indirectly for its revenues. The entrepreneurial system is strongly self-exciting, partly because of the profits that it accumulates, partly because of the penalties which attach to under-production and which 'operates to make every ceiling attained into a future floor which cannot easily be lowered'. The governmental system is also self-exciting, though to a less extent and has a vested interest in the growth of the entrepreneurial system which at present alone sustains employment and the growth of public revenue.

I have already suggested that the system formed by the two is breaking down because it is failing acceptably to distribute incomes, earnings or jobs. Any readjustment to meet this need would give far more power to the governmental partner. Progress in this

D

direction is resisted by all those who still believe in markets sufficiently to fear a further curtailment of their influence. And further, the political drive that might power it is weakened partly because centrally controlled economies have not yet been so successful as to confirm the faith of their supporters and partly because of the general distrust which large institutions, especially large political institutions, have come to generate.

The Politics of Growth

The policies realised by the self-exciting system are still widely supported, because they do at least achieve economic growth. Even in the developed countries the standard of life in the lower ranges of the income pyramid is not so high that those who enjoy it would not wish to raise it, even if everyone, including themselves, had not been conditioned to expect growth as of right. Moreover growth has great incidental advantages. It is growth which has so far kept the mixed economy viable, despite the divergent forces inherent in each of the parties of the mixture. It is economic growth which provides an expansion chamber for most of those ambitious and dynamic men who in other systems—and in ours at other times—have pursued their own wealth and power through politics. Any threat to the principle of growth is a fundamental threat to the system.

But the assumptions on which the policies of growth are based are also breaking down. I have analysed these trends in an earlier chapter. All our concepts of cost and benefit, profit and loss are derived from the assumption that an economy on any scale from the domestic to the planetary can be conceived as a flow of energy and materials from an inexhaustible source into a bottomless sink. All must be revised as this assumption progressively fails.

The only truly productive process in the world is, and has always been, the biosynthesis which sunlight generates on the face of the planet. What we call production is partly the conversion, more or less wasteful and irreversible, of inorganic material, including fossil fuels, into humanly convenient artifacts, including usable energy. For the rest it consists in fostering the process of natural production through farming and forestry and channelling it into more convenient and durable forms. The first has been the archetype of production during the industrial age. It is bound to shrink as it becomes restricted by costs and constraints which have never been counted before. The second will be the archetype of production in the post-industrial age. It will no doubt expand to an extent not yet imagined. The post-industrial world will have different perspectives and its technology will serve different interests. But it is most unlikely to be less 'big business'.

Today, however, these growing doubts about the rightness, even the sanity, of the goals which the system is set to pursue only intensify the doubts with which ordinary individuals view not only the present system but any system formed by large-scale organisations.

The Anti-Institutional Revolt

The institutions of today carry a far greater load than human institutions have ever carried before. Men are more dependent on them and make greater demands on them than ever before. Their performance is far more exposed to view and is judged by far higher standards than before. They are no longer supported in their task by being regarded as part of a natural order and for the same reason their critics are no longer muted. Their tasks have grown to such a scale that even when they attempt them, their beneficiaries have not collectively the knowledge to comprehend them or the maturity to accept them. They have also become involved in tasks as diverse as the devastation of Vietnam and the designing of obsolescence into the motor car, which their beneficiaries rightly reject but which they are at present systematically restrained from changing. Many of their tasks are too difficult to do well, even when they need to be done; large-scale physico-social planning is an obvious example. And ecological changes will soon destroy the conditions which enable them to be done even as well as they are being done now.

It is a daunting situation both for their officials and for their beneficiaries. No wonder it has created a gulf between them. The gulf is natural but its manifestations seem to me none the less pathological.

First, the archetype of the bad official has changed. He is no longer typified by those bad players of good roles attacked by John the Commonweal—the lazy prelates, the grasping merchants, the venal judges. He is Eichmann, the dutiful official whose devotion serves only to further the alien ends of a non-human or anti-human institution. The illustration is extreme but it has its familiar counterparts.

Representatives of employers and labour, exchanging those ethical arguments which I described in an earlier chapter are still half supposed in their official roles to be deaf to anything but the logic of the market or the battlefield. Functional departments of government and of any other large organisation are slow to accept even as constraints the needs of policy generated by other depart-

ments. Even central governments and central banks have limitations to their vision which are sometimes obvious to simple minds
outside the institutional machine.

All this is true but it is even more true of the individual and
notably of the revolutionary. In so far as Eichmann is a cautionary
example, he is so for everyone. Anyone can become the dutiful
servant of a single system to the exclusion of all the others that
makes demands on him. Most commonly he can become the devoted
servant of his isolated self. The anti-institutional stance is an escape
based on deceit. It creates a new antithesis; instead of the good
official and the bad official, we have the official and the anti-
official, that romantic but escapist figure who was born to challenge
the enlightened man but who has survived to conceal from those
who assume his *persona* their own responsibility for playing not one
but several roles.

The counter-culture of the Western world expresses a huge
load of anti-institutional feeling and articulates itself in various anti-
institutional philosophies. All these seem to me to be less important
for the truths they articulate than for those they ignore or deny.

Ivan Illich, for example, distinguishes institutions which enable
man to do things from those which force him to produce and
consume. Postal and telephone services enable men to communicate
but neither force them to do so nor censor what they say. They
enhance individual life. Such institutions he calls convivial. At the
other extreme are institutions which produce and ensure the consumption not only of products like the motor car but of public
services like education and health and welfare. In the view of
Illich all these are manipulative and thus inhuman or anti-human.
Institutions which are not convivial can do nothing useful but set
limits within which human life must be lived.

For Illich 'modern technology has increased the ability of man to
relinquish the "making" of things to machines and his potential
time for "acting" has increased . . . the choice between sad unemployment and joyful leisure is now open to the entire culture'.[4]
But the book from which this quotation is taken has nothing to
say about the forms of organisation which are to provide and work
the machines and to select their products or about those problems
of distribution which occupy so large a part of current institutional
time. He articulates a valid and eloquent protest against the self-
exciting system but gives no indication of the means or the pattern
of distribution which the State's negative powers of proscription
are presumably to impose. Such a political apparatus might possibly
employ fewer people but no one should suppose that it would be
less extensive or weaker or more 'responsive' than our present system.

There is another, more optimistic view of organisations which sometimes blends with and sometimes qualifies the criticisms of the counter-culture. It is derived from the new theories and technologies of communication and it traces the defects of our institutions to their archaic structure. According to this view our existing types of institution are indeed both inhuman and inflexible but only in so far as they still embody the mechanical ideas of an earlier day. Like the dark Satanic mills of the 19th century, they were designed to centralise control, transmit orders and neutralise resistance. The organisations of the future will be designed as nets for the mutual exchange of information. Appropriate groupings for action will emerge in response to the needs of changing situations, and will replace the old rigid hierarchies of power and authority. These institutions, it is claimed, will be neither inhuman nor unadaptive.

The insight is important and valid so far as it goes, but I do not think it goes very far. Our contemporary institutions, governments, businesses, universities, and any other, may still be more auto-cratic than they need be. But no increase in communication and participation will of itself suffice to bridge the gap between us as persons and institutions on the scale which our personal needs require. The hope reposed in it today is today's version of the vision which two centuries ago powered the institutional hope implicit in the French revolution; the hope that institutions which allow free communication between free men will always generate con-sensus expressing a general will.

Making Institutions Work

It seems to me inescapable that the future should require institu-tions even larger and more powerful than today's; and I see no reason to be dismayed at the prospect, even if dismay were a useful attitude with which to face the inevitable. 'Unofficial' men do not compare favourably with 'official' men or 'anti-official' men with either. Roles still have the civilising, restraining, co-ordinating function which they had when human institutions were part of the natural order. They are as ubiquitous now as then; and now, as then, they impose their requirements on the done-by, no less than on the doers.

Even if we take a view as extreme as the view of Illich already quoted, we find ourselves relying on institutions to set limits to human activity. No institutions in the Western world today are strong enough to do the least which that prospect shows to be necessary. None capable of doing so has ever existed in our experi-ence, except perhaps those which unified the British war effort in the later stages of the Second World War. If we accept the fact that problems of distribution must grow more, rather than less, political, we must add to these prescriptive functions the distributive ones described in the last chapter. The dream of universal abundance automatically generated *and distributed* by a robot population is a pipe dream.

Moreover, as these problems of distribution grow larger in scale, the organisations needed to deal with them will also have to become larger. Probably time will not permit us to create and accept powerful regulators of more than national scale, so present national governments, however inept, will have to carry most of the load which the future will generate during the critical decades ahead. The hope that regulative units can grow smaller as problems grow larger is another example of wishful thinking.

So the problem is how societies which may number hundreds of millions can become sufficiently informed and committed to support collective action on the scale they will need, without losing the critical capacity which they will also need to keep their institutions under control. It is a problem which will certainly not be solved by populations of 'existential' men who acknowledge none of the social or economic or political dependence which supports them and who look for their meaning within the experience of their isolated selves. It will require on the contrary highly socialised men, whose responses to the claims made on them by any one of their memberships are controlled primarily by their consciousness of the claims of all the others. They will not be 'other-directed' men, driven crazy by the number of conflicting others who are trying to direct them. But their inner autonomy will be won and expressed by managing, not by denying, the conflicts which these claims will create for them personally. How far a society can raise the standard of its citizens' public responsibility in this direction only time will show. Its best efforts will no doubt fall short of its needs and the shortfall will be expressed, as it is now, partly by mutual coercion and partly by inertia. But the result could undoubtedly be infinitely better than it now is.

This will be an educative process in which the state will have a part—unless we insist on leaving the instruction to disaster. Nothing better illustrates the pathology of our current attitudes to membership and especially to political membership than the paranoiac denial of society's right to 'bring up' each new generation in the awareness of its situation and its needs as 'society' sees them. This includes the need to make its citizens critical—but also to accept the responsibilities of the critic. The fear of this influence has tainted every word in our vocabulary which refers to this process of 'bringing up'. Even education does all it can to escape the implication that it is concerned to develop any specific views or attitudes about anything. It is time to accept the obvious fact that the right of the individual to make up his own mind, to differ, to advance other views only makes sense when seen against the background of a society which has and uses a voice of its own.

A love-hate relationship has always existed between men and their institutions. One pole was expressed two centuries ago by the words—'Men are born free but everywhere they are in chains'. Though nearly all the chains that chafed men as the 18th century closed have been struck off, chains of subservience to nature, gods and other men, the complaint is louder than ever from the prophets of the counter-culture. Our chains are our institutions or the system which our institutions have combined to form; and the jailers are the officials of those institutions by whom those institutions act, themselves doubly enslaved by subordination to their official roles.

The other pole is its exact reverse. Individuals, it declares, are born into and fashioned by an institutional environment which supports them as basically as the air they breathe. They are free only in so far as they are born into the freedoms which their institutions provide. Their main significance and responsibility is to preserve and extend those freedoms, and their main way of doing so is the way they play the roles which their institutions offer to every one of them. They are liberated by their institutions and the guardians of their liberties are the officials through whom their institutions act.

This view also has its contemporary prophets. It is implicit, if not explicit, in every revolution of our century from Atatürk to Castro, from Mussolini to Tito, from Lenin to Mao Tse-tung. Despite their contrasts, all these were inspired by the need both to create an integrated institutional system and to bridge the gulf between institutions and persons by generating a shared enthusiasm for collective achievement and a universal acceptance of personal responsibility for achieving it. Most of them seem to have been more successful at institutionalising persons than at humanising institutions. All of them have been the answers of specific peoples, conditioned by a specific culture, history and circumstance. Answers are always specific; but questions tend to be universal. The answers of the counter-culture to the universal questions, which we, no less than other people, have got to answer, seem so egregiously inept that they seem more significant as symptoms than as answers.

The post-Protestant ethic will indeed be different from the

Protestant ethic. But it cannot fail to be infinitely more demanding and infinitely more austere.

[Based on a lecture given at the University of Keele in November 1971.]

Notes and References

1. Eustace Percy. *The Heresy of Democracy*. 1954. London. Eyre and Spottiswoode.
2. J. K. Galbraith. *The New Industrial State*. 1967. Hamish Hamilton.
3. G. Vickers. *Freedom in a Rocking Boat*. 1972. Penguin Books. Chapter 3.
4. Ivan Illich. *Deschooling Society*. 1971. London. Calder and Boyars.

CHAPTER 7

Institutional and Personal Roles

The Institutional and the Personal

We recognise that the institutions of government and business in America and other Western countries have become so closely interwoven that we may regard them as a system. This system is run by men, but by men playing institutional roles. Their criteria of judgment and their standards of success seem to us to be those of the institutions which they serve. So when the system produces threats which alarm us or wrongs which outrage us, we may conclude that the system's ideas of success are quite different from our own. Some people feel so about the Vietnam war. Many people are equally offended at the way the system distributes incomes, wealth and power.

Apart from criticisms of what it is trying to achieve, we may also become anxious at the system's failure to do even what it is trying to do. We can see that the greatest cities are becoming ungovernable. And when we hear of great enterprises threatened with bankruptcy, we may question whether they have become unmanageable. Like men at sea, we may become anxious either about the course the ship is taking or about its ability to keep afloat, or both. Either is sufficiently alarming.

The managers of every kind of institution are equally familiar with both anxieties. They are expected to keep the institution in being and at the same time to realise the most acceptable mix of all the various things they are trying to do. The goals of balancing and optimising (or even 'satisfying') always conflict; yet the same set of decisions must serve both.

Our present institutions can be criticised both on grounds of responsiveness and on grounds of efficiency. They may need radical change. But unhappily we cannot assume that all our troubles are due to these defects. There are problems which attach to human governance as such and they are mounting. They would be making greater demands on our institutions and on us, whatever our institutions. We have no reason to be surprised at the mounting instability of the system.

The first of these general factors is the enormous expansion of the ethical dimension. The question of who gets what becomes an ethical question whenever the answer depends, or is thought to depend, even in part on human decisions. As our environment becomes increasingly human, so an increasing proportion of our threats and blessings seem to stem from the decisions of other men and so fall into the class about which we can argue that they ought to be different and which we can change, if at all, by the techniques which influence men, rather than by those which manipulate the physical world.

The present storm of ethical protests is largely due, I believe, to the huge expansion of issues which are rightly deemed to be ethical. The wilderness does not owe us a living. Even the market does not owe us a living. But between us and those impersonal worlds is spread an institutional world on which we subsist, all of us as members, most of us also as employees. And all our individual rights as members, even as employees, have an ethical dimension. We can meaningfully argue about what they ought to be.

A second factor is the ambiguity which surrounds the concepts of forecasting and planning when we apply them to human affairs. Nothing human is predictable in the sense in which the movements of the moon are predictable; and no operations on them are plannable in the sense in which moon landings are plannable. Some years back an English study showed that the population of south-east England would increase by 5 million in the next 20–30 years. Plans were proposed for new towns, new highways and so on. But the already overcrowded people in south-east England refused to accept this figure as a prediction. If the towns were not built, the population would not expand. Of course this view, like the other, was only partly true; demographic changes are not wholly obedient to a planner's will. But equally they are not unaffected by a planner's plans or even by a forecaster's forecasts.

A third factor is the growing disparity in scale between problems, agencies and beneficiaries. In 1961 a British minister of transport commissioned a report on urban traffic congestion. The report[1] pointed out that this congestion was not a problem but a symptom of the problem that modern cities generate more activity than they can contain. The smallest system worth studying was the city, not just its roads. Cities could indeed be redesigned to contain more activity than they do now. But any such redesigning would have to take account not just of accessibility by vehicle but of access on foot, safety, parking, amenity and so on; of which disparate and conflicting goods different partial satisfactions were to be had at varying prices.

The problem involves a whole physico-social system. But the agency which commissioned the study was a functional department responsible only for transport. And the people for whose benefit the exercise was being done were concerned with even smaller fragments, differing radically with their position. Those who lived in the restricting houses were frustrated by the encroaching cars. Those who used the encroaching cars were frustrated by the restricting houses.

The example brings out a fourth factor – conflict between the divergent interests of the beneficiaries, bred by this disparity of scale. These conflicts must grow greater as larger scale problems impose larger scale solutions.

So apart from any defects of our present institutions, any future institutions are going to make greater demands on their beneficiaries, who in some capacities must also be their victims—greater demands on their intelligence; greater demands on their breadth of interest; greater demands on their confidence; and greater demands on their ability to reconcile conflicts, including conflicts of role; greater demands in fact on their humanity. As human beings we should not object to that.

But it sets us thinking about the nature and the limitations of these nets of mutual dependence in which we are enmeshed and so about the expectations on which they depend. And this brings us to the ubiquitous concepts of role; because role systems are precisely nets of self- and mutual expectation.

From varied experience of playing institutional, professional and personal roles and reconciling their conflicting demands, I have reached some conclusions which are currently unfashionable.

First, I attach a wider meaning to the concept of role playing than some may find familiar. What I have come to expect of myself and of others and to regard as legitimate expectations by them from me seems to describe a good deal of what I am and what others trust me to be. So I do not hesitate to talk of personal roles, which some people today may regard as a contradiction in terms.

Next, I think of role playing as a creative activity and of role players as agents of change. This is partly but by no means wholly because I have been lucky in playing roles in new and fluid organisations, apart from the role of being myself, which was once more new and fluid than any.

Third, I attach great importance to the element of conflict which is present in all role playing. There is conflict between institutional and personal roles. There is conflict between institutional roles and within each individual role, whether institutional or personal. But this does not frustrate them or make them unplayable. The resolution and containment of conflict is what role playing is all about.

Finally, I have learned from personal experience, as well as from observation, that the capacity for resolving and containing the conflicts inherent in roles varies with the role player, no less than with the role. I am thankful that there should be men and women willing and able to play, even badly, all the roles I cannot play at all.

I should add that I have lived a long life in a country where the level of internal conflict has been lower and the level of trust, especially trust in officials, has been higher than it commonly is in America. So I assume as possible and even normal some ways of resolving and containing conflict which some Americans may have come to regard as impossible or even undesirable. The contrast may serve to remind us that the limitations of social and political life are functions of the state of specific historic societies at a particular point in time. The limitations might be even narrower and the possibilities are surely greater than anything any of us has yet experienced.

I am also impressed by the extent to which my country, in the last seventy years, has been not merely adaptive but creative in the field of human values. Its operative standards of what human relations are acceptable and unacceptable have greatly grown and changed; and on the whole I approve those changes. The span has had its moments of abysmal stupidity and dishonour; but so, in retrospect, has mine. It is at the moment in a trough of some confusion and disillusion, faced with regulative challenges that it cannot meet and with intellectual and moral problems that it cannot solve. So am I. There is nothing in that to alienate me from my institutions. I think no worse of my country's development than of my own. Those who are not constrained by so humble a view must make allowances for me.

Some Conceptual Innovations

For two millennia Western philosophers have been debating the relations of the individual and society or of the individual and the State. The problem is an artifact of our culture. In traditional societies the social dimension comprises both the political and the personal. As the development of our societies bred, on the one hand, gigantic political and economic organisations and, on the other hand, atomised individuals, so the gulf which this fission created demanded an explanation. It is no less a problem for being a cultural artifact.

In the last century or so, psychologists, sociologists and cultural anthropologists have joined the debate, to refine or confuse the underlying assumptions about human nature, human thinking and human values. I have neither the time nor the competence to link all I have to say with that huge volume of conflicting authority. But it may be useful to mention some conceptual changes which have marked the last thirty years and which should have influenced all of us who regard our education as still continuing.

About thirty years ago scientists began formally to distinguish information from energy. This was a major conceptual revolution. For nearly three centuries the physical sciences had been almost wholly absorbed in disentangling energy from matter, with which at the end of the 17th century, it was still utterly confused. Thereby they had answered some important 17th century questions, such as the nature of heat and light; and they had established the continuity of organic and inorganic processes and of human life with other forms of life. But they had hardly begun to explain the *differences* between men and other animals, because they had hardly begun to explain organisation in terms of information, still less in terms of shared individual response to information, which is the essence of human social life. To distinguish information from energy as a means of inducing change, still more as a means of preserving form, set scientific minds free from the shackles of their most recent success, though it did not thereby break the habits of many lifetimes.

Ethologists, comparing the human with other species, established some useful similarities. It is useful, for example, to remember that, as I stressed earlier, men are biologically social but not biologically political animals. The largest societies which have supported them through more than ninety per cent of their existence as a species have been loose associations of families. Men have depended on men since men were men; that is how they became men. But human societies have not depended on each other until a few centuries ago. The reminder is useful but it tells us nothing about human possibilities. Our peculiar gifts for creating, through communication, a common conceptual world, have enabled us to create societies different from those of other creatures. Whatever be the limitations on making a planetary society, they are likely to be no less specific to our kind.

In view of the course which scientific thought had taken, it is perhaps inevitable—though I think it is unfortunate—that the greatest stimulus to new thinking about the differences between men and other creatures should have come neither from the bio-logical nor even from the psycho-social sciences but from physicists, mathematicians and communication engineers, designing neo-mechanical systems. The common factor in these is that they are designed to hold some set of relations constant or to a prescribed course—first, thermostats and automatic pilots; then self-directing anti-aircraft guns; then automatic factories, homing missiles and space probes. These stimulated a lot of theoretic, especially mathe-matical thinking. They also generalised in common usage new words and concepts, such as feedback, which were to prove conceptually important. Our ways of thinking are always much affected by the machines we use.

One idea which was to prove curiously liberating, though it seems so obvious, is the idea of the mis-match signal. A pilot, whether human or mechanical, responds not to the changing com-pass bearing but to the *comparison* of that bearing with a given course. The same compass reading will have a different meaning for him, if the course is changed, because the effective signal is generated internally, by comparing the incoming information with an internal standard.

This shows that information is an incomplete concept. It implies a receiver capable of being informed. Its meaning, if any, depends on the organisation of the receiving end—for the automatic pilot, on the course. This, however obvious it may seem to non-scientists, is a more sophisticated idea of a signal than many psychologists had allowed themselves for fifty years. It does not mean that all the work on conditioned responses is wasted labour, or even that all the current work on exciting the so-called pleasure centres—or are they addiction centres?—is wasted labour. But it does insist on the obvious fact, so constantly ignored, that human beings are systems regulated at different levels, by different regulators which often conflict. And it stresses the importance, when dealing with the more human aspects of personal and social—and equally of institutional—behaviour, of identifying the internal standards which give meaning to information, and the ways in which these standards grow and change.

The design of man-made control systems has been made possible by the computer; and this new tool has also had conceptual side-effects for good and ill. On the credit side, it has made visible a category-difference between a computer and a programme which no longer frightens communication scientists; so I hope it will in time encourage the more timid psychologists to draw a category distinction between brain and mind at least not less wide than that between hardware and software. On the debit side, it tempts us to beat our problems into a shape that our computers can handle and thus further encourages the delusion that scientific and technological problems are typical of human problems, which they are not.

To design a bungalow is a problem different in kind from designing the first atomic bomb and basically much more complex. The difference is that for the Manhattan project the criteria of success were simple and compatible, whilst for even the smallest bungalow they are multiple and conflicting. Scientific questions are 'why?' questions. Technological questions are questions of 'How?' or 'How best?' where the criteria of 'best' are given. But the simplest policy question is a question of what *is* best, where the criteria of 'best' are multiple and conflicting and their relative weight is just what has to be decided.

These questions have given new authority and direction to the study of systems of all kinds and especially of social and political systems. System concepts have long been familiar in other fields, notably in biology. Early last century Claude Bernard, impressed by the advantage gained by those creatures which had developed means to keep their blood heat constant, coined his famous statement that 'the stability of the internal milieu is the condition of free and independent life', a statement which has extraordinarily wide applications.

From the 1940s onwards people have been becoming ever more conscious of other fields in which systemic relations are important to them. One of the earliest to be noticed was in the ecological field, at first in the local phenomena of soil erosion and consequent dust bowls. Today mounting pollution, wasting or committed resources and multiplying populations combine to form an obviously unstable system of enormous size which cannot go on for long as it is going now, and so invites regulation to achieve some pattern even slightly less repugnant to our human values than that which it will otherwise take. The example helps to make clear what the regulative function of government really is.

Again, the economic system is increasingly seen as part of a socio-technical system which not only links men as consumers with men as producers but also conditions men as members of society. So we increasingly accept that it needs and admits of regulation in accordance with multiple, conflicting standards, within the limits imposed by the need for 'stability'.

For there is a difference between the biological norms studied by Claude Bernard, built-in, stable and changeless over many generations and the norms that regulate personal and social and political systems. These are multiple and conflicting. They operate to achieve and preserve not just stability but the most acceptable combination of relations that can be reconciled with stability. They often jeopardise stability in the process.

When I compare the intellectual world in which I have lived for the last thirty years with the world in which I grew up, the changes are remarkable. Matter has ceased to be material and machines have ceased to be mechanical, as those words were used at the turn of the century. Stability, not change, demands explanation; and the explanations we look for are in terms of communication, rather than of energy transfer. Communication is limited not by the means to send messages but by the organisation at the receiving end; and this consists of historically generated standards by which incoming information is interpreted and without which it would not even be noticed. Energy, mankind's most ancient limitation, is for the moment superabundant, and so are the means for sending messages. But the means for interpreting messages are in total confusion; and in consequence all the relations on which human life depends, at every level from the planetary to the personal, in every aspect from the economic to the ethical, are in danger of dissolution, because the regulative standards on which they depend have become confused or polarised in conflict.

So the major threat at every level is the lack of what I have called an appreciative system[2] sufficiently widely shared to mediate communication, sufficiently apt to guide action and sufficiently acceptable to make personal experience bearable. The major need of collective existence at the moment is to generate such a system. The aspect of that system with which I am concerned in this chapter is the net of self- and mutual expectations which mediates our mutual relations.

Self- and Mutual Expectations

No one, I think, will question that, whatever else we learn, we learn what to expect; and that men differ from other animals partly in the variety and assurance of the expectations that they learn to build. I will return briefly to the distinction which I have already drawn between our expectations of other people and our expectations of the rest of the natural world; and also between our expectations of each other and our expectations of ourselves.

We are born into a world of people. We develop expectations of them which we confirm or revise in the light of experience; but we also do all we can to make them behave in the way we would like to expect. They do the same to us. The staggering success of the result is hidden from us only because we take these expectations for granted, until they are shaken.

We also develop expectations of ourselves, partly but not wholly by acknowledging the legitimacy of other people's expectations of us. It is these which make our behaviour more predictable than that of a bird on a bird table. They develop a personality on which other people can rely. These self-expectations may be more or less or other than what others expect of us. We need to distinguish— and we do—between what we do because we think it well to comply with what others expect of us and what we do because we expect it of ourselves. Both, but especially the second, give us the experience of self-regulation.

If we did not have these self-expectations, we could not have the same sort of expectations of other people. We assume that they are regulated in the same way; and in varying degrees, we assume that we know what their self-expectations are. With a close friend, the assumptions we make may be wide, detailed and confident. With strangers they become more attenuated. Members of a close but functional body, like a ship's company, are usually linked by a net of self- and mutual expectations which is exceptionally firm and detailed but in an exceptionally narrow context. With those remote from us in language, culture, or experience the net of assumption is weaker. But it is seldom wholly absent. I find it curious and encouraging that it should transcend cultural differences even so much as it does.

I stress the importance of this net of self- and mutual expectations because I wish to distinguish it from those more general expectations on which our other external relations are based. The brain and central nervous system can recognise and abstract regularities in experience and use them for prediction at levels far simpler than the human. Thunder presages rain. Night follows day. Human prediction based on regularities such as these is familiar and impressive. From the measurement of the year which made agriculture possible to the measurements which guided the last Apollo landing on the moon, the human mind has systematised its experience of the natural order so as to guide its expectations with impressive scope and accuracy.

This, however, is in the field of natural science which Herbert Simon recently and most usefully distinguished from what he called the sciences of the artificial.[3] Natural science is knowledge of what would be as it is if men were not here to know it. And though what men can know of it must bear the imprint and limitations of the human mind, our knowledge of it is different from our knowledge of other human beings, because we have personal experience of being human.

The sciences of the artificial are wider than the psycho-social sciences. A steam engine is a human artifact, explicable only in terms of human purpose. Michael Polanyi[4] has been insisting for many years now that, though we can explain a broken crankshaft in terms of metal fatigue, we cannot explain the crankshaft itself except in terms of the human purposes for which it was designed. But I am not concerned to pursue the science of the artificial in that direction. I want to focus on the fact that all dealings of men with men are made possible and conditioned by a network of expectations which each has of the others and of themselves and by assumptions of each participant about the self- and mutual expectations of the others. Next I want to enquire what part this net plays when human relations transcend the personal and become institutionalised.

I have already stressed the dependence of all societies on rule and role. Unlike a rule, the criteria for a role cannot be fully and explicitly defined. The role player has a discretion and a duty to exercise his discretion within his role. In an effective organisation, each member trusts the others to do so and to extend the same trust to him. To take a very simple example, in all the English versions of the game of football,[5] a player often has to choose between whether to pass the ball or try to make progress himself. If he sticks to the ball and fails, his fellow players are quick to judge whether he was in breach of his role or only unsuccessful in achieving a legitimate intention. There is no room in a team for a player who is either too selfish to play his role honestly or too unskilful to play it acceptably; but the two judgments are quite different. A breach of role is likely to be more unanimously identified and more violently condemned than an act of incompetence, in a business organisation or a government department, no less than on a football field.

The example is simple but its importance is general. Members of organisations are expected to exercise discretion within limits precise enough to allow others to exercise their discretions but not so precise as to exclude adaptation, learning and experiment. They are traditionally bedevilled by two types—the buck-passer, who leaves his discretions unexercised; and the insubordinate, who commits other people's discretions and sabotages their decisions if he does not like them. Our current ethos prefers the second. Before we accept this view, we should reflect on its history.

Traditionally, in all civilisations, men have used official seats of power to enrich themselves, advance their friends and torment their enemies—in other words, as enhanced opportunities for playing personal roles. The harnessing of private men to public roles is a social and civilising achievement of the greatest importance. And its present extension is perhaps the greatest achievement of our culture.

For as I have already noted, the modern world which Maine described as the transition from status to contract was in fact the transition from a world of inherited status to one in which positions, with their attendant status and roles, could be transferred by contract; and not only transferred but designed and created. Our facility for creating organisations of such variety for any purpose, for designing the most complex distributions of power, vested in positions whose holders can be selected and changed at will – this is a novelty. It is this which has accustomed us to the skills and restraints of institutional role playing and which has made possible the huge institutions on which we depend.

And it is this which has produced in our day a revulsion against official role playing quite different in emphasis from that which marked previous ages. We are no longer afraid of the man who uses his official position to feather his private nest. We are afraid of the dehumanised institution, made even more inhuman by the devotion of its officials.

If we do not believe in the justice of our laws, we shall not be proud that they are enforced without fear or favour. If we think that our defence institutions are endangering and dishonouring us, we shall not be comforted to reflect that their officials are playing their roles honestly. If we think that profit-making institutions have a built-in interest inconsistent with that of the consumers they serve and the workers they employ, we shall not be reassured by the reflection that their officials are serving that interest successfully. If we think that trade unions have a built-in need to escalate the inflation that threatens their members, derived from a built-in duty to protect them against it, we shall not be sustained by knowing that they are doing that duty devotedly.

Similar doubts can be honestly if not always validly entertained about universities and even about student organisations.

In such situations the first need is to examine the communication networks, internal and external, which serve the policy making machinery of the criticised institution, and consider whether and how this can be made sufficiently responsive to the needs and wishes of those whom it affects—*all* those whom it affects, not only its critics. We may conclude that it cannot be made so responsive, either because it is locked into an exclusive relationship with one or more special interests or even because it has become independent of all the interests it is supposed to serve and serves only its own self-generated purposes, possibly only its own survival and growth.

At this point we may be tempted to generalise and assert that *all* institutions develop standards of success which are alien to the persons whom they should serve, and that *all* officials of institutions are depersonalised by the mere fact of playing an institutional role and are thereby disabled from exercising any criticisms of their institution's policy. Eichmann will then indeed become the symbol of officialdom. Official roles will appear as the antithesis of authentic selfhood and we shall have to choose between withdrawal and endless war on all institutions.

The last step in this familiar sequence is always, I believe, a slide from the challenging through the defeatist into the absurd. To make and keep institutions responsive and responsible may indeed sometimes need radical and abrupt change, sometimes necessarily from without as well as from within. But the art of institutional role playing will be needed to work the new institutions no less than the old; and it is in fact the main innovative and creative agency of peaceful change.

Changing the Institutional System

The conflict between personal and institutional roles varies with the situation. I was dramatically reminded of this at the end of the First World War. On the morning after the armistice, the commander of the division with which I was serving pointed out to his battalion commanders that the object of the exercise had changed overnight. The war being won, their role was to ensure that the potential civilians under their command passed their time until demobilisation as usefully and pleasantly as might be. They should therefore form soviets, as the Russians had recently done, and invite them to think out and organise their activities. (The word was new; the Russian revolution was less than a year old.) They should remember that discipline, relaxed in some directions, would be more demanding in others, notably in relations with the French civilian population on whom we were billeted and who no longer needed in their midst these huge concentrations of foreign armed men. I have always remembered with respect the sensitivity of that regular soldier to the effect which a change of situation would have on institutional and personal roles conditioned by four years of war. It worked like a charm and saved a lot of trouble. It would not have worked a week earlier.

Changes of situation seldom solve our problems in that way. They usually demand the pursuit of goals even further from the natural implications of personal roles than those of their individual constituents; and they sometimes demand the change from without of institutional structures too rigid to change themselves. An English banker in Shanghai, when the communists first took over, observed with admiration that their soldiers no longer pillaged the civilian population and that their judges were no longer venal. That change was brought about by a revolution. I would suppose that for the most part new men, with new conceptions of their roles, were holding the old positions. But these reforming roles were more, not less institutional. As soldiers, as judges, as revolutionaries, the new men had developed self- and mutual expectations which could subdue the variety of their personal standards. An immense institutional conditioning produced that cultural change.

I had personal experience of an institutional change which, though legally effected, was revolutionary in character, in that an intervention from outside replaced one system by a different one at short notice. The Act which nationalised the British coal industry created a new public board, to be managed by eight men, and transferred to it the assets, the contracts and the employees (numbering three quarters of a million) of more than six hundred private companies. The Board was told to get the coal, organise the industry and satisfy the consumer; duties never before expressly laid on anyone. It was to cover its costs from its proceeds; but this requirement of financial stability was a condition, not a criterion of success. Success was to be measured by comparing its achievements with what informed opinion thought it might have achieved in the dimensions of its new public responsibilities.

In principle there is nothing new in this. It is, for example, the way we measure the success of a City government in traffic regulation, sewage disposal and all the other diverse and conflicting fields which it is required to regulate. It makes clear but does not create the conflicts which exist—and which ought to exist—between the various goals of every organisation. There is some necessary conflict between the interest of producers and consumers; between the technical task of coal getting and the equally technical task of conserving the surface; even between the interest of different classes of user of a single type of coal, produced in different places at necessarily different cost. The interest of the exercise lay in the process of generating a new role system in an organisation new both in structure and in express purpose, yet consisting almost entirely of individuals trained in the previous system. The opportunity was created by legislative intervention but the changes were produced by the mutual communication of men holding new or changed positions, inventing and discovering, learning and teaching each other new roles. This was partly a conscious process, speeded by deliberate techniques which I need not describe here.

The newest element in the system was the requirement, imposed by statute on the Board, to consult with all the employees on all matters of policy. This involved role relationships which were most unfamiliar to most of the personnel in the industry and indeed elsewhere. Its possibilities and limitations remained to be discovered. Its potentialities for good and ill were very great Its actuality, I believe, was great and almost wholly good. It was a heartening experience of the creative possibilities of role playing in a sufficiently unstructured situation.

Now consider a third example, where the initial impulse towards institutional change came from within. In 1951 a social worker in a London teaching hospital (she was formerly a nurse but had been invalided out of that profession) reached a climax of discontent with her role. Hospitals, she felt, had become so obsessed with cure that they were neglecting care, especially the care of terminal illness. This surely was a betrayal of their founders' intentions and of the proper role of medicine, which is the management, not only the cure, of illness. It also impeded, rather than helped, the dying to make dying a significant experience. But what could one woman do, practising her profession in an institution designed to frustrate its proper exercise?

The answer depends partly on the woman. This one gave up her job and her profession—she was then aged 33—and qualified as a doctor. Then she got a grant for research in the control of intractable pain and made a reputation in that speciality as a physician in a cancer hospital. Then she took enough time off clinical and research work to raise half a million pounds and build a 70-bed hospital to her own design; and became its director. By that time she was 49. The hospital[6] has been running now for almost seven years. It will soon have 100 beds, which is as large as she wishes it to be. But in co-operation with the local general practitioners, it is already treating in domicilary care as many patients as it has in its beds. It is building a teaching unit; and it handles more than 1400 visitors a year. So many different sorts of people came to see and learn.

Her main role conflicts now are between therapy, administration and teaching. But at least she has solved for herself the conflict that drove her out of her profession into a medical school twenty years ago. She has solved it also for all who work in her hospital. She has articulated the problem and one solution on such a scale that it is heard and considered at the policy making levels of our national health service and in other countries.

And in the course of all this she has 'done her own thing', which was concerned neither with nursing nor with doctoring as such but with the significance of dying.

That is one way of reconciling a personal with an institutional role.

There will probably never be more than a small percentage of people who have as much of what it takes as Dr S. Those of us who have less must do the best we can. She might have practised her ideas as a social worker outside a hospital. She might have escaped the personal conflict by getting out of the field altogether, into a dress shop or a travel agency or a market garden. She might even have stayed put and stilled the nagging mis-match signals by learning to be a passable organisation woman—not a good one, because a role player who cannot both innovate and criticise without being false to his (or her) role is less than good at the job. Any of these courses might even have been the best *for her*—if it had been the best she could do. Most of us may have to put up with such compromises. But let us not suppose that the best we can do is necessarily the best anyone could do.

Bearing the Institutional System

What we cannot change, we have to bear, as lesser people than Dr S. have borne, the conflict that she resolved. But bearing is a far from passive affair. It can make a difference.

Though Dr S.'s dilemma was one which only an exceptional woman could solve so well, it was relatively mild by the fearful standards which this century has set. The most evil and yet most strongly self-supportive system of this century was, I believe, the system which possessed Germany from 1935 to 1945. It is there, if anywhere, that we may expect to find examples of individuals imprisoned in institutional roles that denied them humanity. So we do; and the denial affected also all of those who became engaged in trying to destroy that system. But even in the darkest corners of that dark system, there were surprising gleams of light.

Occupied Holland at the end of the last war was acutely short of food and mass starvation threatened when the Allied advance cut off the populous centres of the West from their supplies. At that point the British high command received through underground channels an invitation from the German chief of medical services in Holland. Four British doctors should be sent to Holland at once to prepare to take over the administration of famine relief and to help in arranging Allied air-dropped supplies for civilian relief before the war ended. Instructions were added for getting the doctors in. Four British doctors joined German headquarters in Holland, while the battle was still raging; and the shambles of transition later was a little less in consequence. The German who took that weirdly risky initiative partially resolved a role conflict in a way which would not have seemed feasible, if he had not shown that it was.

There were even more rigid institutional traps—for the commandants of Jewish labour and death camps. Viktor Frankl,[7] an Austrian doctor and psychiatrist who spent most of the war as a prisoner in Auschwitz and Dachau, ended it in a smaller camp to which he had volunteered to transfer to deal with an epidemic of typhus. When the camp was liberated, three Hungarian Jews seized the commandant and hid him in the woods. Then they sought the commander of the liberating American division and offered to give him up on one condition—the general's personal assurance that no harm should come to him. The puzzled general agreed; the commandant was given a job in organising relief; and when time permitted, facts were found that justified the prisoners' odd response. The only medical supplies the camp had had for months had been bought by the commandant in the nearby town with his own money, through intermediaries sworn to secrecy. The rapport between him and his prisoners had developed unerringly through a tacit communication network most dangerous to both.

I have arranged these examples on a descending scale—descending towards the point at which a bad institution extinguishes the possibility of good personal initiative. There is one lower rung on this dismal and frightening ladder. What of the prisoners, enmeshed for years in a system designed to dehumanise them?

Frankl expresses his conclusions with alarming simplicity. There is, he says, only one question worth asking about the meaning of life. It is addressed not by men to life, but by life to men. The question is—'What does this situation require of you?' To this question, says Frankl, there is for every respondent always one and never more than one right answer, which is accessible to anyone willing to do the work needed to find it. Correspondingly, there are always alternative answers which for that respondent would be wrong. Human initiative is never exhausted.

I would not venture to express so stark a faith; but I respect Frankl's and I take some comfort from it. Life has not yet questioned me so sharply as it questioned him.

The Personal Role

I wish to challenge the escapist, defeatist and irrational illusion, so sedulously cultivated today, that integrity, even 'personality', can only be expected to flourish in those who can elude the challenge of institutional roles, whilst they depend unavoidably on our institutional world. These challenges cannot be avoided; even the role of beneficiary (or victim) is an institutional role, containing a discretion of critical importance to the institution and the individual. Nor should they be avoided, because they are among the more important of the tensions involved in the making of a personality.

I am not alarmed at regarding the making of a personality as the creation of a role. It offers wide discretion in the making; but as it develops, it is as demanding as any other role. Is not a person a *persona*? If we say to someone—'What you have done was not like *you*', are we not appealing to a set of expectations which he, by his past actions, has invited us to have of him and which we in consequence expect him to have of himself?[8]

A personality is a personal creation, controlled like any other work of art, by its own developing logic. It generates its own rules, possibilities and limitations. The supposed antithesis between the determinate and the arbitrary is, I believe, a fallacy, generated by carrying the concept of linear causation into human life, to frustrate at every level our understanding of the process we call self-determination. The dynamism and the direction of this process are provided by the constant need to resolve those conflicts which are endemic in all our systems of self- and mutual expectation.

Among those conflicts we are today especially conscious of the conflicts between institutional and personal roles. Institutional roles can indeed be dehumanising. So can anti-institutional roles, notably the role of the revolutionary. And so can those personal roles which evade the challenge of the institutional world by opting out of conflict with it to a greater extent than their own limitations require.

But any world which generations younger than mine may create or preserve on the other side of the dark decades ahead will include an institutional dimension and will make the same demands on us as players both of institutional and of personal roles. It will generate the same tensions and will require at least as much mutual trust as ours today. No organisational panacea will relieve any of us of the duty to sustain those tensions or to generate that trust. Institutional roles may impoverish or enrich us; and so, as they develop, may the personal roles which are so much a part of our personalities. But equally, both are our opportunities for making ourselves and our societies. Men without role conflicts would be men without roles; and men without roles would not be men.

[Based on a lecture given at the University of California at Berkeley on the invitation of the Institute for International

Studies in April 1971; published in *Human Relations* Vol. 24, No. 5, and republished by the University.]

Notes and References

1. *Traffic in Towns.* 1963. H.M.S.O. (The Buchanan Report.)
2. In a series of writings I have developed the concept of an 'appreciative system' to describe the interconnected set of largely tacit standards of judgment by which we both order and value our experience (e.g. *The Art of Judgment*, Part I, 1965, London, Chapman and Hall; New York, Basic Books. 1968, Methuen University Paperbacks. *Value Systems and Social Process*, Part III. London, Tavistock Publications; New York, Basic Books, 1971. Penguin Books, 1972). I find this formulation more comprehensive than that formulated by Professor Kenneth Boulding in *The Image.* (1961, The University of Michigan Press) and more exact than 'consciousness' as used by Professor Charles Reich in *The Greening of America.*
3. Herbert A. Simon. *The Sciences of the Artificial.* 1969. Massachusetts Institute of Technology.
4. Michael Polanyi. *Personal Knowledge.* 1958. Routledge and Kegan Paul; and many later writings.
5. I do not know the American game well enough to know how far this is true of it also. Those familiar with the English versions notice with surprise that the American game admits of tactics explicitly formulated during the course of the game.
6. St Christopher's Hospice, 51–53 Laurie Park Road, London, S.E.26.
7. The incident is recorded in Viktor Frankl: *Man's Search for the Meaning.* 1962. New York. Washington Press.
8. I have developed this idea further in *Freedom in a Rocking Boat.* 1970. London. Allen Lane, The Penguin Press. esp. Ch. 6. *Men Without Roles* also (1972), New York Basic Books and paperback by Penguin Books.

CHAPTER 8

Of Bonds and Bondage

The Ambivalence of the Bond.

Human beings are social animals, dependent on each other. Practically and psychologically they need to rely on each other. A human society is a tissue of reliable relationships, far wider than can be created by personal kinship or friendship or by express agreement. The most pervasive element is the expectations which attach themselves to defined positions of all kinds and the roles associated with them. The more familiar and important they are, the less we notice them, especially when they are negative. We assume that the stranger will not prove to be a robber, that the shopkeeper will not prove to be a cheat and so on. We are lucky. These nets of expectation on which we rely are slowly built and easily destroyed.

The word 'rely' is derived from a verb which means 'to bind'. Our reliance is on a set of bonds, which bind us to each other. The word bond is a reassuring word suggesting a pledge which is not to be broken. Friendship is a bond. Even a promise to pay is an invitation to trust and a testimony to trust.

But bondage to another man or to an institution—that is another matter. No man or institution dare claim that it has another man in bondage. And those who feel that they are in bondage admit no restraints to what they will do to break their 'bonds', and evoke widespread sympathy and tolerance in their rebellions. The right to revolt against 'bondage' is among the strongest and most widespread ethical standards of our day.

It is curious that two words of such similar origin should have developed meanings so antithetical. The explanation I have already given. Our bonds are what we expect of ourselves and trust others to expect of themselves. Our bondage is what others expect of us and can elicit from us by coercion but which is not accorded by our own self-expectations.

Our expectations of others are based on assumptions we make about their sense of obligation, however derived; and theirs of us depend no less on their assumptions about the network of obligation tacitly assumed by us. We and they know well enough what others will expect of themselves in the ordinary situations of life and will consequently accept as the reasonable expectations of others. We rely on each other in so far as we are bound to each other by these nets of assumed mutual obligation.

To the minds of the Enlightenment the past condition of mankind seemed to have been a *triple* bondage: to nature, gods and other men. Freedom from want, superstition and tyranny seemed all that was needed for human felicity; and all were attainable by human reason. More specifically, technology and the division of labour would free us from want; science would free us from superstition; and democracy would free us from tyranny. This grand simplification has had its day and achieved its results, for good and ill. We need today a much more sophisticated concept of our condition.

What the 18th century described as 'bondage' is in fact a complex pattern of limitations. The laws of nature are as they are; they are to be accepted, not re-made. And though greater understanding of them has opened the huge possibilities of technology, this also has its limitations, as we begin to realise through our dawning understanding of human ecology. Science has dispelled many superstitions but it has only made visible the limitations of our understanding. Democracy has overthrown many tyrannies but it has not reduced the need for human governance. On the contrary, in all three fields the effective limitations are increasingly set by men; and the burden of 'bondage' grows greater as men become increasingly dominated by human decisions which they do not accept. The pursuit of those freedoms which dazzled Western Europeans 200 years ago has brought their descendants up against a single limitation—their ability to meet the much higher demands which they have been led to make *on each other*.

The boundary between bonds and bondage fluctuates constantly. A slow trend generates claims which are first felt as bondage and later accepted as bonds. English noblemen are no longer irked by the fact that they cannot defend their honour with duelling pistols or claim priority on the highway by virtue of their rank. An opposed trend, spasmodic and violent, leads some generations to define as bondage what its fathers accepted as bonds. Uncle Tom's bonds are bondage to a Black Panther. These two movements reflect a recurrent theme of this book—the conflict between the claims of multiple loyalties and the inherent human desire to distinguish simply and tidily between a recognisable coherent 'us' and an undifferentiated alien 'them'.

Political democracy, a market economy and the contractual role have combined for two centuries to mute these ethical conflicts. We should not underrate these blessings which we have enjoyed so long and which we are now to lose. 'Laissez faire, laissez passer' promised *and gave* far more than economic expansion and the chance of personal wealth. It promised and gave some freedom from ethical frustration. It established a social milieu towards which it was both possible and legitimate to behave as to the natural milieu. It was based on most modest human expectations; the economic man was only a hungry rat. We know its social and ethical shortcomings. We should not forget that these very shortcomings muted the social and ethical claims by each on all which would otherwise mount, as they are mounting now, to produce—despite rising affluence and equality—relations more likely to be felt as bondage than as bonds.

Drawing the Frontiers between Bonds and Bondage

How does the individual develop these standards of self-expectation which determine which relations he will accept as bonds and which he will reject as bondage? The more obvious part of the process is indoctrination by his society—*every* society to which he belongs. Unconsciously, if not consciously, every human system encourages in its members those attitudes which its members believe to serve its survival and the pursuit of all it is set to attain. It thus encourages them to accept as bonds what would otherwise be bondage. These expectations may be more or less agreed and more or less universal. In feudal England, and still more in traditional India, roles were highly diversified, widely agreed and relatively unchanging. The title of a paper *My Station and Its Duties* in J. H. Bradley's *Ethical Studies* reflects how completely Victorian England still accepted the idea that life was ordered in hierarchic stations, the responsibilities of which were bonds, not bondage. The title sounds vastly old-fashioned today but it is our age, not the Victorian, which is out of step with history. Societies today consist of a pattern of 'stations' far more complex and interdependent than ever before and depend as much as ever they did on the occupants of those stations doing what their stations require. In a contractual society the occupants of these stations may change more often. In a fluid society their roles may change more rapidly. In a complex society their roles may conflict more fiercely. All these changes make more difficult the playing of the roles attached to every station. But they do not relieve in the slightest degree the dependence of society on its role-holders and of them on it and on each other.

What societies teach is one thing; what its members learn is another. The voice of society is important but not all-important; and its importance varies with several factors.

First of these is the unanimity and confidence of the instructing voice. The child hears first the voice of the family; soon the voice of school and the peer group and the mass media, these last earlier in their impact now that they no longer depend on ability and willingness to read. All these voices consciously and unconsciously expose admired, censured and ridiculed types of human action, character and thought and invite the child to internalise them. The persuasion which these voices combine to give may be more or less *coherent, comprehensive* and *apt*. In so far as it is self-contradictory, it either enforces a polarised choice or breeds only confusion. In so far as it is not comprehensive it leaves areas unstructured by any standard except such as the individual can make for himself. In so far as it is inept, it invites the recipient to notice the contradictions between its precepts and what society actually does or between its precepts and what the situation obviously requires or both.

But by far the most important way in which the persuasive voices may vary is in the extent to which they encourage autonomous judgment by the recipient. Is the admired type blindly obedient, rebellious on principle or responsibly critical? And in what areas of thought or behaviour is rebellion or criticism most encouraged or repressed? These are the differences which chiefly determine whether a culture will ossify, dissolve in chaos or successfully mediate growth and change.

The child is at first a captive unit in a small society. From its earliest days it is encouraged, deterred, *conditioned* by the adult world around it. How far and how soon will it differentiate into a unique system, structured by self-expectations far from identical with any of those which its social milieux have tried to make it internalise? The answer depends partly on how far its individual experience has in fact been different from those of others; and this in turn depends partly on genetic factors and partly on the variety of experience which the society offers, notably the varieties of income, role, education and culture of its children's parents. Societies which aim consciously to inculcate the attitudes of membership seek to make these backgrounds uniform or to formalise their differences in rigid castes. By contrast, the highly classified but 'meritocratic' societies of the West as they exist today are particularly apt to ensure for their children backgrounds both diverse and confused. They subject them to a stream of persuasion which is peculiarly incoherent, non-comprehensive and inept. And they stress with more confidence than any of their other instruction the need and duty and capacity of the individual to form autonomous judgments on any subject. It is not surprising that these societies should today be experiencing what a recent writer called a vacuum of loyalties; in other words that their members should be more conscious of bondage than of bonds.

I have repeatedly stressed the dependence of modern societies on members capable of sustaining the demands of multiple membership. I believe this is equally essential as a condition for the growth of individuals in all the significant dimensions of humanity. It follows that *education for multiple membership* is far more important and far more difficult than ever before. It is time to lay aside the dominating suspicion of societal influence on the individual, especially where the societal influence is exerted by the State. The real situation is far more complex, more difficult and more demanding. All claims by authority, like all claims uncontrolled by authority, need to be considered critically. But the authority of the democratic State is at least more responsible and more accountable, as well as more essential than most of the other authorities to which we are subject; and the growing constraints which it imposes are the measure of the growing assurances which it offers. Its voice is none the less only one of the 'inputs' which are 'processed' by the strange crucible of the individual mind.

The individual has to organise himself; to impose some kind of order on the incoming stream of his experience. For the means to do so he is utterly dependent on the social milieu into which he is born. The very language he learns contains implicitly some elements of order, besides being his main instrument for ordering experience. But his own task is unique to him. He has to learn to act effectively on and in his own small world, to communicate with his fellows and to keep his experiences hearable to himself. He discovers how far the world of his experience corresponds with what he is taught to expect, how far the standards which he is urged to accept are accepted by others, how far they accord with his own character and capacities and how well they work in his own limited world of action and communication and experience. In his search for identity he rejects what he cannot assimilate and pursues what he comes to need. His process of self-determination is in principle not unlike the process which develops and changes his society, and indeed all the other human systems of which he is a member. It is an integral part of that process. But it is unique to him and it determines, amongst other things, his relation to them.

The individual *chooses* whether to regard life's demands as bond or bondage and his choosing is a kind of learning. He cannot choose what those demands shall be; but to some extent he can anticipate them. The future is unpredictable because we cannot tell how men will respond to its demands. But the demands themselves are often clear enough.

New Bonds—or Bondages?

I have already described some of the inescapable demands to which people in Britain, and in varying degrees men elsewhere in the developed Western world, will have to respond as best they may. They all follow from the need to establish a viable relationship between rights and responsibilities, political, economic and social— in other words between the constraints and assurances of all our memberships. Since everyone is going to depend increasingly on assurances derived from membership, everyone will have to accept increasing constraints derived from membership. The need is inherent in the claim. It may not be met, but if it is not met, the claims will not be met either.

We may be sure that these constraints will be regarded first as bondage. The question is whether they will come to be regarded, sufficiently widely and quickly, as bonds. The transition will be an act of social learning. If the analysis so far is substantially right, it is easy to summarise the main directions which this change will have to take. It will involve accepting:

1. A massive change in earning differentials in favour of labour-intensive activities.
2. A more radical adjustment of all net earnings in favour of more equitable incomes.
3. A cut in total net personal incomes to meet the amount by which the demand for more resources for investment and for collective use exceeds any possible increase in productivity. (Much of this shift will be represented not by greater results but by the need to do more work to attain the same results under greater constraints.)
4. A stabilisation, if not a cut, in personal expectations.
5. Confinement of competition as a regulator to the shrinking field in which winners can afford to be indifferent to the plight of losers.
6. The value and nature of 'order' as a necessary though man-made condition of human life and of the process and time scale within which it can be changed.

7. A large extension of the boundary between self and other and between present and future.
8. A more realistic concept both of equality *and of inequality*.

These changes will not take place quickly or painlessly or even adequately. In so far as they are inadequate, the resulting 'order' will be inadequate, costs will be higher, benefits will be less and both will be differently spread. In the next three chapters I examine the process by which we manage conflict and its relation to the processes of social learning. For these are manifestly the processes on which we depend for the survival of everything we value. Before turning to them I will comment on some current responses to these needs. I have already suggested that social learning in Britain in the last seventy years has not been unimpressive. I believe that it was never so fast as now.

The first three of the changes summarised above are aspects of that huge exercise in national budgeting which I have described in earlier chapters. I observed that the people of Britain as I wrote this are in the undignified position of refusing to both their alternative governments the means to control the inflation which most disturbs them. I do not mean by this that nothing is *happening*. I have already insisted that every human act is also a communication and is often more potent as a communication than as an act. The Labour administration in Britain in 1964–70 failed to introduce either an effective incomes policy or an effective influence over trade union activity. But it started a debate among its supporters and in the country which made such action thinkable and discussable. The legislation of its Tory successor gave another stimulus to the debate. I have no idea how this debate will look by the time these words are printed. Such debates may result in polarised conflict, no less than in consensus. But however it results, it will illustrate the truth that political action and social learning are processes distinct but closely linked and that the visible results of the former are seldom so important as their unidentifiable effect on the latter.

I have already suggested that proposals for the reduction (not the *relief*) of poverty, whether by way of negative income tax or of social dividend, are potent as communications long before they become effective as acts. Negative income tax is on the face of it a mere administrative device, devised by a right-wing economist to simplify schemes for supplementing income. Its potency as a communication lies in the fact that (perhaps even more than schemes for 'social dividend' distribution) it expressly acknowledges the role of political membership in adjusting everyone's total personal income and provides an explicit and flexible way of expressing the

E

current standard of what the relation between incomes and earnings should be. We should not underrate the importance of such communications. The Beveridge report was written to terms of reference which called only for a more economic way to administer existing services and was so little expected to raise political issues that apart from its chairman the committee which produced it consisted wholly of civil servants. Yet it was the most potent ideological instrument produced in Britain for half a century.

Furthermore, the debate on how to eliminate 'poverty' will, I believe, reveal that this will not break the vicious mutual relation between unemployment, inflation and the inequitable relation between earnings in the capital-intensive and labour-intensive sectors or even achieve its own objective until that relation is broken by other means. It may thus open up for discussion the proposals I put forward earlier in Chapter 3, or other proposals equally radical.

The fourth and fifth of the changes listed above are closely linked. Escalating expectations for all mark the last phases of a predominantly competitive culture. Here again the limitations of competition are beginning to force themselves on the attention of citizens as they are expected to feel an increasing concern for each other and at the same time to compete in the market for the shrinking resources of jobs and land. The second is at the moment an even more dramatic object lesson than the first. Economists have always known that market regulation applies only to commodities of which the supply increases in response to an increase in the price offered for it. Not everyone is yet convinced that people, our only abundant resource, are becoming too expensive to be used. But anyone can see that the land surface of a small island cannot increase in response to the rising demands of its multiplying inhabitants. It would be approaching the point at which a market ceases to be a suitable distributive mechanism, even if speculation were not multiplying the rate of its escalation.

I wish I saw greater signs of this fact leading to effective social learning. The legislation current as I write this aims in the limited but most important field of housing to meet the escalation by subsidising rents. This will reduce some distress and reduce some anomalies but it implies a belief in market regulation for a commodity which has ceased to be responsive to price. It surprises me that those who boggle at nationalisation of land should not already have proposed to replace the concept of beneficial ownership in land by the principle of trust.

It is already established that the owner of land cannot do what he pleases with it, but he is still regarded legally as a beneficial owner, subject to an increasing number of largely negative constraints. It would be neither irrational nor particularly difficult to convert his status into that of a trustee, entitled to benefits as manager and perhaps also as tenant of trust property. The idea that the property owners of Britain 'own' the island is not a readily acceptable one, even though half the homes are owner-occupied and even though government departments, including the Forestry Commission are by far the largest landowners.

The rights and responsibilities of trustees have been particularly well developed in English law. It is perhaps the greatest English gift to international jurisprudence. If, as seems clear to me, the market, however limited by planning controls, has ceased to be a suitable, and will soon cease to be a viable means to adjudicate between competing land uses and land users, a first step towards sanity would be to establish the principle that all landowners are trustees for the public and for posterity and that whatever they earn is to be justified as a reward for managing a trust estate. Merely to debate such a proposal would be a potent instrument of ideological change —more potent perhaps, because less easily rejected than proposals for State ownership.

The sixth and seventh changes listed above are more subtly linked. I have already analysed the manifold results which followed when men ceased to believe in a divine or a natural order and made themselves the architects of their own societies. *Any* effective architecture today, as I have argued, requires wide consensus on plans with long lead times and distant time horizons. But, equally, *any* effective architecture requires the self-appointed architects to keep a roof over their heads while they rebuild. Law-and-order has become a dirty expression. It is in fact the first and greatest gift which political organisation gave to the weak against the strong. Its demands, whenever it is seriously challenged, will always take precedence over all others in the minds of the great majority of men, except in political situations very remote from any which face any Western country today. Here again, social learning is active in Europe as well as in North America.

The eighth change—a more realistic concept of equality and inequality—though the most essential is the least in evidence today. Economically we live in a society in which earnings, incomes, wealth, power and status are still distributed in far from equal ways—some, like inheritance, the fruit of ancient tradition; some, like trade union negotiation, the fruit of very recent theory and practice. I have already expressed the view that necessity if not mutual sensitivity will make greater equality acceptable. But no conceivable changes in the direction of equality could meet the current egalitarian ethic or could take place so long as that ethic is dominant. Its absurdity is reflected in the contemporary odium attaching to the word 'élite'.

We take pride in the fact that most positions in our society are filled by selection on merit, rather than by birth or favour or self-imposition. Their occupants are *chosen* and are, or should be, *choice* specimens, better in that context than those who have not been chosen. This is precisely what an élite should be. No sane person reaches maturity without becoming aware of the dimensions in which other people excel him, often dimensions in which he himself most wishes to excel. In physical and mental endowment, in practical, ethical and aesthetic judgment, in courage, initiative, endurance and sensitivity he can see around him examples to emulate, even though he knows he cannot equal them. His ideas of equality should start from and accommodate this awareness. And so should the ideas of each individual among those different élites on whom our world will increasingly depend. When this degree of realism penetrates the consciousness of today's democracies, they will be ready for tomorrow.

For every shift towards economic equality *increases* the importance which individuals will attach to the status attached to their positions. These positions need not be hierarchically ordered in terms of respect. I have never found it difficult to admire skills I do not possess (and, often, could not have learned) whether the excerciser were earning more or less than I; and I do not suppose that I am peculiar in this respect. The fact remains that each individual in tomorrow's society will remain alive (as he does today) by right of political membership, usually supplemented by employment in a position for which he has been *chosen*. This pattern of membership and employment will constitute an *order*, changeable indeed but a datum at any given moment. And those who make up the pattern and depend on it for their life from day to day will have to accept and respond to its demands, even though they know that it is a human artifact and even though they are committed to changing it. If such a pattern of élites is a pattern of inequality, then we shall have to learn to live with inequality, with none of the traditional supports to sustain us in the process—except intelligence and respect for our fellow men.

As I have argued earlier, the concept of 'order' as a human artifact is expanding dizzily. It now includes virtually the whole of the physical and social environment, including much of those standards and attitudes of our own which make us the social environment of our neighbours. And the area thus consciously planned cannot fail, I think, to go on expanding. In time this might, I believe, provide a world of greater and more varied satisfaction and assurance, individually no less than collectively. In the meantime the question is how far the constraints and assurances of political membership, subjective as well as objective, can be made to grow to the measure of each society's need.

This is a learning process and like all learning processes, it is speeded by three interacting streams of experience—the individual's experience of event; of his fellows' communication; and of the results of his own reflection. Although the three are obviously inseparable in practice, it is useful to distinguish them because each has its own limitations. Experience even of the most widespread national disaster bears differently on each individual. Each participates in a different small section of the huge resonating web of communication; and each is limited by his own capacity to organise his own experience, to empathise with the experience of others and to appreciate those aspects of the huge flux of events which constitute his own contexts and situations.

We can reduce these limitations by deliberate policy only to a small degree; but this is none the less important and might be decisive. The greatest solvent of mental limitations is a dramatic change in circumstances—consider how easily, willingly and completely Britain accepted the demands of war-time organisation. Apart from war, the changes in circumstances which threaten us, though equally radical, may not be so dramatic. So even more attention should be focused on public debate, the second major change agent in a process of peaceful change. And since the effect of this in turn is limited by the training, as well as the gifts, of the adult minds which participate in it, we need an assessment of what can reasonably be hoped from more relevant education. The remaining chapters are contributions to these themes.

PART III

Education for Multiple Membership

CHAPTER 9

The Management of Conflict

The Ambiguity of Conflict

I have often recurred to the theme that human societies survive only so long as they can resolve or contain the conflicts which they generate. This is especially important at a time when the level of conflict, both external and internal, is rising so rapidly as it is now, and when accepted means of resolving and containing it are showing such manifest signs of overstrain. So it is timely to explore these three concepts—*conflict* and its *resolution* and *containment*. They are important, imprecise and distorted by some inadequate ideas about them which history has bequeathed to us.

We use the word conflict in two very different senses. We use it of any situation in which the parties involved are constrained to decide between alternatives none of which is wholly acceptable to them all—or even when a single individual or collective decision maker has to resolve a similar dilemma. We use it also of the hostilities which erupt when such conflicts can be neither resolved by 'acceptable' means nor contained within 'acceptable' limits. What constitutes acceptability remains to be explored.

During the last war, for example, the shortage of food in Britain created a conflictual situation, in that there was not enough to satisfy all demands. Yet people did not fight each other for food. The conflict was resolved and contained by a rationing system, centrally administered and popularly supported. There was not even a substantial black market in conflict with the rationing authority. In consequence the distribution of food caused virtually no conflict in the second sense and was perhaps more equitable than it has ever been before or since.

The example is worth exploring for the light it throws on 'acceptability'.

Before the war our society relied largely on market mechanisms to determine the volume and price of the food supply. Nearly everyone relied for their daily subsistence on the assumptions that they would have enough money to buy at least their minimum needs, and that there would be enough food in the shops to satisfy the total effective demand. Neither assumption was necessarily true. The first was imperfectly sustained by supplementing incomes in accordance with principles which had been badly shaken by the depression of the 1930s. The second collapsed with the limitation on imports imposed by the submarine offensive and the needs of war. In a situation where rising prices could not elicit larger supplies of food, market distribution would have caused escalating prices and profits to suppliers and would have starved all but the rich. This would in time and in theory have immobilised the work force. In fact, of course, long before starvation could have had this effect, resentment at the inequity of distribution would have caused a change in policy or, failing that, attacks on food stores, food distributors and the most favoured classes of recipient, and these conflicts would have had quicker and more disruptive effects than the starvation which they would have anticipated.

The alternative solution introduced by rationing also rested on unspoken assumptions—that the State could mobilise enough competent and honest employees to administer the scheme; that the public would accept the need for it and co-operate sufficiently to make it work; and that the reduced food supply could be kept at a level which would be sufficient for all basic needs. If any of these conditions had failed, conflict in the second sense would in time have erupted between the worst pressed and the least pressed or between the worst pressed and the state or both.

Thus the point at which conflict degenerates into conflict-in-the-second-sense is a function of several factors both objective and subjective.

Once a conflict passes this critical point, it becomes a threat to the system as such, not merely to its present state; and thereupon it changes both its parties and its nature. It changes its parties by mobilising on one side all those who rally to the defence of the system, whatever their attitude to the particular dispute, and on the other, those who declare their indifference to the system in so far as it impedes their preferred solution or even their hostility to it because it does so. It changes its nature because those who become thus divided are almost bound to re-define each other as aliens or as enemies, at least so far as concerns their former common membership of that system. They thereby exclude each other from that part of their environment to which they acknowledge or expect any duty. And the mutual relations within which they might have resolved or contained their differences will be disrupted by this change, perhaps irreversibly. International and civil wars are familiar examples of this crossing of a threshold. They have their counterparts in industrial relations, personal relations and perhaps even in the psycho-pathology which results when such conflicts can be neither resolved nor contained within a single head.

Such thresholds are a common feature of systems of all kinds. They mark the point, not always predictable, at which the system's capacity for sustaining itself is overwhelmed. The result may be that the system wholly disintegrates or that it re-forms in some more or less changed shape. How far, in the second event, its successor is to be regarded as a new system or as the old system changed depends on what aspects of the old system are regarded by the observer as most essential to its identity.

My purpose in this chapter is to give a more definite meaning to this threshold in the context of political societies.

The Sources of Conflict

The constraints which give rise to conflictual situations are of three kinds. Some I will call logistical constraints. There is a limit to what we can do, limits which can be only roughly estimated, within wide margins of risk and uncertainty. Moreover, resources are limited. Aspirations, even when not mutually inconsistent, compete for scarce resources. This scarcity cannot be remedied by increased abundance, partly because time and attention, most essential of resources, cannot be expanded, but also because scarcity is a *relation* between our resources and our aspirations. However rich we are, we can spend money, life, time only one way. So the more choices we have, the more we have to say 'no' to.

So conflictual situations are increased, rather than reduced, by the growing powers of men to manipulate the physical world. And today these conflicts are further increased by a new factor. Multiplying populations, wasting resources and mounting pollution are making it evident that the greater our powers, the less we can afford either to use them or to restrain them without counting multiple and disparate costs. There could be no better illustration of a conflictual situation.

A much more dangerous source of conflict is the constraint necessarily imposed on us by the wishes and expectations, no less than the acts of other people. These constrain us in two ways, of which the most conspicuous today seems to be the constraint of 'authority'. Every society and organisation to which we belong has its expectations of us and can bring pressure to bear on us to comply with those expectations. It also has its own powers of collective choice, which commit us, whether we agree with the way they are used or not. These are the powers of *authority*. In societies which become increasingly organised, and especially in pluralist societies which pride themselves on the multiplicity and independence of their institutions, authority is bound to be an ever increasing source of conflictual situations.

Individuals, societies and organisations of all kinds, in so far as they are *not* constrained by some common authority, constrain each other no less by the pressures they use to influence or restrain each other's initiatives and even by the mere fact of exercising their own. In an increasingly crowded and interdependent world, these mutual constraints also are bound to mount. Indeed, the need to resolve or contain them is one main reason for the extension of authority. Yet in so far as authority assumes more responsibility for resolving or containing such conflicts, it tends to raise correspondingly the level of tension between it and those who are subject to it.

Most Westerners today are more apprehensive of constraint by 'authority' than of constraints by each other. This balance could change—I think it will and should. But wherever it stands, constraint will flow both from all the authorities to which we are subject and from all the initiatives of our fellows which authority does not control. Both are mounting and must continue to mount.

The resultant escalation of conflict (in the first sense) is not of itself dehumanising. On the contrary, conflictual situations are the hallmark of human life. Their resolution and containment is the basic art of being human. It is what distinguishes a man from a bird on a bird table. Birds fly, feed, preen, mate, fight in sequences measured in seconds, each dominated by a single impulse. Every human choice, by contrast, whether it be deciding on a family holiday or settling a national budget, or even a wage claim, involves balancing through time a host of disparate criteria, not all of which—usually, not one of which—can be fully satisfied. The mark of a successful individual or a successful society is that it manages to sustain *through time* a host of different relationships, keeping each in accord with some standard of expectation, whilst containing all within the resources available; and developing all these standards in the process. These developments are easy to see when we look back over the history of any field of social policy. Progress in the human dimension depends on increasing skill in resolving and containing conflict.

So we should not be surprised by the need to increase this skill. We should not even be dismayed, unless it seems to make demands which cannot be met or which can be met only at what would seem to be some unacceptable cost. And this is of course the threat which dismays us today. For conflicts are best resolved and contained where the parties share strongly what I have called the constraints and assurances of membership; and this is precisely what is hard to generate on the scale and in the conditions of today, except at costs which we are accustomed to regard as unacceptable in the highest degree.

This brings us to the third area in which conflictual situations are generated and without which conflicts in other areas would be neither resolved nor contained—or even noticed. This is the organisation of our individual personality systems. We develop not only conflicting fears and aspirations but also more or less conflicting standards which define what we come to expect of ourselves in all our manifold contexts. These introduce conflict into our personal situations. The making of a reasonably coherent personality is a task which few accomplish in a lifetime. And even those who do so experience continual conflict between the demands of the various roles they play, as well as within each of their roles.

Moreover, the state of our individual personality systems determines what conflict, if any, will be involved for us by the constraints of the natural world and of society and of the independent agents around us. We may recognise what others expect of us and deem it prudent to comply. But the degree of conflict in the situation depends on how far their expectations of us correspond with our expectations of ourselves.

Finally, the skills involved in the resolution and containment of conflict are in the last resort personal skills.

So the organisation of individual personalities is not only an independent source of conflictual situations but also the key factor in determining how all conflictual situations are perceived, resolved, contained—or not contained.

The three kinds of constraint which I have described are reflected in three familiar verbs. What we can and cannot do, must and must not do, ought and ought not do to are defined by the constraints imposed on us by circumstances, by other people and by ourselves. Each of these constraints can raise conflicts. Each conflicts with the others. And any or all of them may conflict with that simpler category, what we want and don't want to do. I will not pursue further here the permutations of this matrix of potential conflict or its psychological implications; but nothing less, I believe, is adequate to represent the variety of potential conflict inherent in human relations at every level from the personal to the planetary.

Levels of Conflict

I need next to distinguish four levels at which conflictual situations may arise in a society. The first is the level, already distinguished, which does not involve authority. Individual citizens may bicker within the wide limits set by the law and social tolerance. Political parties and trade unions may feud with each other, and so within them may the members of each. Departments of businesses, no less than of governments and universities, may engage in venomous in-fighting. I shall usually be little concerned with this level, because any such conflict must usually escalate to the level at which it involves 'authority' before it breeds one of those destructive exercises which rank as conflicts in the second sense.

In conflictual situations involving authority, we need to distinguish three further levels.

Every society has its own rules for settling conflicts, including rules which allot responsibility for decisions. The first level of conflict takes places within these rules.

But these rules themselves are open to change and are indeed in constant change, partly through the pressure of dissatisfaction generated by their earlier application. The second level of conflict is concerned with the changing of the rules by which the first level is contained. This is the level of most political activity. A century ago, for example, the right to pursue industrial disputes by strike action was just being established by changes in the criminal law of conspiracy. Today controversy about changing these rules concerns the need to ensure the contestants' public responsibility, rather than their private power.

But the power to change the rules is itself subject to restraints, legal, constitutional and conventional; and these form a third level of possible conflict and one which is especially important to my subject. It is the pride of democratic institutions that they provide constitutional means to change the rules and even to change a written constitution. But the histories of most democracies include periods when the pressure to change the rules used highly irregular procedures, from civil disobedience to armed revolution, from violent mass protest to personal communication through dramatic forms of murder and suicide.

Disputes at these three levels involve authority and its office holders in different degrees and even in different ways. At the first level authority is neutral. The conflict does not challenge the existing order. At the second level the existing order is challenged, though not 'order' itself. The attempt at re-ordering is still 'orderly', but it is more likely to engage representatives of the existing order on one side of the conflict. At the third level, authority is necessarily engaged as a principal in the dispute, since it has a primary duty to preserve the system's accepted means of growth and change and to resist attempts to impose or oppose change by other means.

Types of Conflict

It is useful also to distinguish conflictual situations according to what the conflict is about. Three types can be distinguished though they are always found in combination.

The type least easy to recognise and hardest to resolve involves conflict about what the situation shall be deemed to be.

To a planning authority a decayed urban area is a threat to a number of sanitary and other standards which the authority has a duty to maintain. It is at the same time an opportunity to reshape part of the physical environment to meet more adequately the changed requirements anticipated ten years hence. The two requirements conflict. This conflict, however, is not visible to most of the residents in the area. To them 'the situation' is a variety of current shortcomings in dwellings and facilities, by no means the same as those which most worry the authority. The criteria which they apply to any proposed change are the benefits promised in terms of these shortcomings and the costs which these would involve in terms of current inconvenience and disturbance. Benefits expected ten years hence have little power to offset costs expected now—and no power at all to do so, unless the residents can learn to attach reality to that view of the situation which is natural to the authority.

An interested developer, on the other hand, has no difficulty in seeing the situation on the same time scale as the planning authority. Even if he sees only a site ripe for profitable development because of its currently depressed value, it may well be easier for him to understand the situation as seen by the authority and the wider criteria which they apply (even though he does not share these) than it is for those who live in the place.

Even on the authority there will be some councillors who see the situation primarily as the need and opportunity to improve the accommodation of specific ill-housed people, whilst others regard the expected increase in site values as a better criterion or the meeting of future needs. So the differences about what the situation shall be deemed to be express and are affected by differences about the values to be attributed to different criteria of success. And even where agreement exists about the aspects to be included in the situation and about the criteria to apply, fierce differences may still arise about the best course to take. Of the alternative development plans submitted to the authority no logical deductive process can *prove* which is best even by the criteria agreed.

Disagreements about how the situation shall be seen and how it shall be valued are so intimately connected that I find it convenient to describe the two together as differences of appreciation. Conflicts about how to attain agreed ends, though they bulk so large in studies of decision making, are always subsidiary to appreciative problems and seldom, if ever, raise irresolvable conflicts between those who are at one in their appreciation of a situation.

All major conflicts involve differences in the values which different parties attach to different aspects of a situation common to them all, differences which often lead them to different definitions of the situation itself.

Some writers have tried to resolve this by distinguishing an in-built hierarchy of importance in the values which men and societies seek to realise. I view this distinction rather differently. It is true that some *situations* define a single criterion as being of overwhelming *urgency*; but when this happens, human initiative is at its nadir. Central and local governments, for example, like business enterprises, need to remain solvent; and when threatened with insolvency, they have to cut their expenditure to match their revenue before the course of events cuts it for them. In such emergencies cuts fall wherever they will be most immediately effective. A logistical constraint has become dominant. The system is threatened by the impending failure of one of its *conditions*, just as the performance of a statesman may be threatened by lack of food and sleep.

The example reminds us that social, like individual, human systems, are partly hierarchic. Their higher functioning depends on sustaining the stability of lower levels. But these underlying stabilities are only *conditions* of higher-level success. They neither assure that the government or the individual whom they sustain will perform his regulative functions 'well' nor supply any criterion for determining between good and bad performance of that function.

Sometimes the situation attaches overriding importance to some function which is not apparently in such a basic relation to the hierarchy. An impending breakdown in traffic control may create an emergency in which the threatened relation has to be given top priority. But here again the explanation is the same. The impending breakdown would affect the functioning, even the survival of the system as a whole and claims priority on that ground alone. It reflects no priority inherently attached to the relationship as such.

It is important to distinguish this hierarchy of urgency, especially as it is so frequently manipulated by those who wish to increase the importance which others will attach to some particular relationship. But it seems to me to throw no light on the procedures by which we resolve or contain our endemic conflicts in those conditions where we have some scope for initiative.

Conflicts between rival criteria are sometimes distinguished from simple conflicts of interest. The distinction, I think, is fallacious. A conflict of interest is simply one in which differences about the definition of the situation and choice of relevant criteria derive more obviously than usual from the position of the parties. They merit attention none the less because they have been taken as typical in both recent and earlier models of conflict and its resolution.

Models of Conflict

Our understanding of human conflict has suffered, I think, from our readiness to think of it in terms drawn from much simpler areas of experience, such as mechanics or ethology or game-playing. I have no space here to examine these models adequately but I need to define one limitation which is common to them all.

Our earliest models are mechanical. Rival demands or views are conceived as *forces* which, impinging at different angles with different strengths, produce not a result but a *resultant*; sometimes movement corresponding to a 'resolution' of these forces; sometimes the 'breaking' of the 'weaker' structure involved in the collision. These analogies ignore the fact that human beings, even in the crudest opposition, influence each other primarily by communication, rather than by the transfer of energy. Even the bombs dropped at Hiroshima and Nagasaki were—and were intended to be—more effective as communications than as agents of destruction.

More recently the study of conflict in other species disclosed rituals for 'containing' conflict and led some ethologists to compare our species unfavourably with stags and wolves. When like is compared with like, it may be held that the human species' democratic methods of choosing leaders are more humane and more effective than trial by combat. But the real difference lies in the much higher level of communication involved, which renders the attraction of followers more important than the elimination of potential rivals.

More recently still the analysis of game-playing and especially the scientific handling of risk and uncertainty has clarified strategic thinking and acknowledged the part played in human conflicts by the power of each party to build up for itself a representation of the other's strategy. But it is a characteristic of games that the rules and the criteria of success remain constant at least for the duration of the game, whilst in human life these are precisely what the major conflicts are about.

I would not belittle the contributions which these models have made to our thinking but none of them seem to me remotely adequate. Human conflict is an exercise in communication even when it is prosecuted with bombs and bullets. And it can have the chance of being adequate only if it can be prosecuted at a level very much higher than bombs and bullets.

The concept of 'levels' of communication is one to which communication theorists can now attach some specific meaning; in particular some of them are prepared to describe with precision the difference between 'dialogue' and those lower levels where each participant tries to manipulate the others, whilst remaining unchanged himself. Dialogue no doubt represents only a small fraction of the exchanges which constitute deliberate communication—itself only a small fraction of the total body of communication. To call the political process a dialogue is to flatter it.

Nevertheless even a society the size of Britain does develop, within a single lifetime, views of itself and its situations more comprehensive, realistic and widely held; more exacting standards of what should be acceptable in internal and external relationships; more sensitive awareness of human variety and human need. And these changes are in part the product of mutual communication at a level much higher than that at which words are used as weapons. So we should not be surprised to find similarity, even identity, between the conditions which favour dialogue and those which favour the resolution and containment of conflict.

The Restraints and Assurances of Membership

Persons in conflict, whatever divides them, are usually also related through common membership of one or more systems; and this may impose on them some restraints and give them some assurances which they would not otherwise feel. This factor is of very great importance both to the resolution and to the containment of conflict. I refer to it as the constraints and assurances of membership or for brevity, as the membership factor. It deserves to be examined in detail.

The constraints of membership stem from those three sources which are also the source of our conflicts. They may arise from an objective appreciation of a common situation. Men at sea, for example, even when in open mutiny, may remain aware of their common dependence on the ship and, in extreme danger, may abate their conflicts sufficiently to co-operate in keeping it afloat. Examples no less cogent are implicit in the situation of Britain, dependent for half its food on imports from abroad and even in the total dependence of the human race on the resources of a small and misused planet.

The constraints of membership may also arise from an objective assessment of the expectations sustained by others and by authority and of the results of disappointing them. A ship's crew is subject to ship's discipline and a seaman's knowledge of the sea and of the conditions which it imposes may make acceptable a discipline which would not be acceptable ashore.

Finally, the constraints of membership may stem from what we have learned to expect *of ourselves* in response to the situations in which we find ourselves as members, in so far as these reinforce the constraints imposed on us by the situation, by other members and by authority.

The assurances of membership spring from the same sources. The sailor is assured that other seamen will read the same message from the ship's predicament and will know, as he himself does, the expectations held of him by his fellows and by authority and the cost of disappointing them. And he can sometimes assume that they expect *of themselves* what he expects of himself.

But constraints based on *self*-expectations and assurances based on trust in the *self*-expectations of others differ from the other constraints and assurances that I have described in ways of the utmost importance, which are often overlooked. They and they alone create those bonds of responsibility, loyalty and mutual trust without which human societies neither function nor cohere in face of any serious challenge to their integrity. A mutinous ship's company might conceivably co-operate to save the ship, even though bound to each other by nothing but obvious present danger; but their co-operation would not outlast more than the most acute phase of the emergency. Much more striking is the extent to which men *disregard* their most obvious common interests when they lack the common loyalty and mutual trust *corresponding to those interests*.

As I write, the miners of Great Britain on official strike have withdrawn nearly all safety and maintenance labour from the pits which are their livelihood and are allowing the pressures of the earth to destroy their workplaces, perhaps irrevocably. These are men conspicuously noted for loyalty, responsibility and mutual trust; and the enterprise on which they are now engaged makes great demands on these qualities and has made even greater demands over the long past in which those loyalties were forged. But this enterprise is not the getting of coal. It is the prosecution of an ancient dispute against parties who have changed and multiplied through the long century of that endemic conflict. The system which claims their allegiance at this time isolates them from the other systems of which they inescapably form part—the country, the industry, even their own pits.

Hence the enormous importance which attaches to this distinction between the subjective membership factor of loyalty, responsibility and mutual trust, and the constraints and assurances to be derived from an objective assessment of the situation and its demands. The subjective membership factor determines which of the multiple claims of membership we shall accept and powers our revolt against those which we do not accept, however inescapably we may be involved in them.

We all belong to many systems; far more than have ever claimed the allegiance of men before our day. Some are hierarchic. Political states, federal and even unitary, comprise many foci of loyalty of smaller scale and often with longer history and greater power; and they are themselves systemically related to each other, however lacking their common loyalty and mutual trust, through common dependence on 'spaceship earth'. Other large organisations, notably industrial and occupational, present a similar hierarchic structure. Community of race, religion, education, profession and economic interest cut across these hierarchies and establish between their members systemic relations often of great supportive power.

All these memberships make partly conflicting claims on us. It is not surprising that the structure of our loyalties, even among the most mature and informed of us, should not measure up to this pattern of demand. It is none the less the greatest danger of our time. For all our means of resolving conflict and nearly all our means of containing it depend on preserving among the disputants a pattern of loyalty and mutual trust roughly comparable with the structure of the multiple memberships involved in the dispute.

Force and Violence

In so far as conflicts are not contained by the constraints and assurances of membership, they can only be contained by impotence or by coercion, by which I mean the *threat* of injury. Not all forms of threat, whether mutual or unilateral, are banned by the rules of most societies but most are so banned, because threats between fellow members are in themselves inimical to the constraints and assurances of membership and are likely to escalate into more extreme threats or into attempts to put the threat into action. But authority, banning coercion among its members, assumes the responsibility of enforcing its own ban and thus saddles itself with the difficulties which attend all exercises in coercion.

A century ago, it was widely supposed that political authority rested largely on the coercive force of sanctions. Later a more sociological view recognised the extent to which both law observance and law enforcement depend on public acceptance of law and of the legitimacy of the lawgiver. Both views are valid and both can be illustrated in any society. But they correspond to two largely incompatible attitudes to authority. The members of most societies are sharply divided between those who feel themselves to be consenting members and those who feel themselves to be alien, if coerced non-members.

This divide is expressed in every society by the startlingly different attitudes to force and violence, two words which, though similar, have come to have deeply different connotations.

Political authority has always commanded force, to which some dissident individuals have always responded with violence. To the system member, force, however disliked in principle, is redeemed by being at the service of responsible power, whilst violence is the epitome of that anarchy which authority exists to suppress. To the dissident, violence is the expression of individual freedom against enslaving authority, whilst force is violence debased by being institutionalised. Violence as distinct from force has played and still plays an important part in revolutionary theory and in the revolutionary mystique. Force, on the other hand, has become a more equivocal concept in politics, partly through failure of the sublime self-assurance which once justified its use, partly in reaction against exaggerated notions of what it can do and partly through a new appreciation that force exercises its greatest and least predictable effects as communication, rather than as act.

These irreconcilable views of force and violence are rooted in two different views of political history. One sees the State as the entrenched preserve of a ruling class and a fount of injustice against which lovers of freedom and equality have always a right, if not a duty, to rebel. The other sees it as the embodiment of the ordering process by which the weak are enabled to coexist on relatively equal terms with the strong. Both views are true and the tension between them is probably inescapable. But the more seriously democracy takes itself and the better it succeeds, the greater is the support which it is likely to generate for the second view and the more anachronistic seem the attitudes and slogans of the first.

Anachronistic though they be, our inherited tendencies to suspect force and condone violence when opposed to force are deep rooted.

'God forbid,' cried Thomas Jefferson, 'we should ever be 20 years without such a rebellion . . . what country can preserve its liberties if its rulers are not warned from time to time that this people preserve the spirit of resistance? Let them take arms . . . The tree of liberty must be refreshed from time to time with the blood of patriots and tyrants.' The implication that the users of force must be tyrants, whilst the users of violence are probably patriots rings out loudly after two centuries presumably devoted to disproving it. More disturbingly, it is audible in Britain today.

In fact the credentials of force are at least better than the credentials of violence and the weak have today, I think, far less to fear from it. But though authority usually commands more force than the potentiality of violence opposed to it, it works under a handicap which exponents of violence are quick to exploit. Force is of very limited use *for the purposes for which authority exists* and is hard to use even within its limited scope without impairing authority's remaining armoury; whilst for the negative and simplistic purposes of revolution or even mere protest violence is apt and adequate.

In brief, the regulation and containment of conflict depend today on a level of communication so high as to be doubtfully attainable even in a society which knew its importance and was dedicated to its achievement. To block such communication by violence is easy. To preserve it by force is difficult in the extreme. Yet the essential role of force is to preserve the conditions within which such communication may be possible.

The Resolution and Containment of Conflict

I can now attempt a brief account of the ways in which conflict is resolved and contained. I have already stressed the central part played by rule and role. Roles define what is to be expected of the holders of defined positions by others and by themselves, notably including those positions which carry responsibility for decisions in conflictual matters. They thus express and help to generate those self- and mutual expectations which I have described as the main agents for resolving and containing conflict. They are partly the product of the process which they regulate, because of the element of discretion which they always contain; and they are thus a principal agency of change.

Roles long antedate the existence of any authority capable of enforcing them. Cornish tin miners in neolithic times could not have traded with seaborne visitors, unless both they and the strangers had been able to distinguish with some assurance the roles of trader and raider. None the less, the web of mutual confidence could not have attained even its present tenuous consistency, especially in a society in rapid change, but for two inventions, one of which is political authority on the scale of today. The other, less remarked but not less remarkable, is what I have distinguished as the contractual role.

In traditional societies positions and their roles, political, social and even occupational, were relatively fixed and their tenure depended far less than in contemporary societies on contract terminable by either party. Our current freedom to devise new organisations, and new positions, even new organisations with new roles and to appoint and dismiss their holders is, as I have already noted, a social invention of great importance. One of its merits is that conflict between such role-holders can often be resolved by changing a role-holder. He can resign; he can be dismissed. Conflict is always far more intransigent between parties who cannot escape from their mutual relationship. This is, of course, a conspicuous feature of political societies, which can neither choose nor rid themselves of even their most disruptive members. Indeed, they can do so even less today than in earlier days. And similarly, as frontiers close, even their most dissident members can less easily change their political allegiance or simply go elsewhere. All these rigidities are growing and are likely to grow.

So the load mounts on that mediating factor which I have called the constraints and assurances of membership and especially on its subjective element, which is the main source of responsibility, loyalty and mutual trust. This, the membership factor, operates with very varying degrees of potency in human systems of different types and sizes and even in the same system at different periods in its history. It is normally far more potent in small systems united by a common objective (such as a team of explorers or even a professional partnership) than in a diffuse political society or even a large business corporation. However strong or weak, it improves the system's capacity to resolve and contain conflict in at least three ways. In so far as it makes the operation of rule and role acceptable, it *mutes* potential conflict so that it scarcely arises. At the other extreme it helps to *contain* even the fiercest conflict by reinforcing whatever sanctions authority commands. For dissenters cannot rebel against any specific decision without challenging the system as a whole and awakening the opposition of all who feel protected by it. Moreover, the would-be rebel cannot pursue his rebellion without putting himself out of membership of his society, re-defining his former fellow members as aliens or enemies and correspondingly re-defining himself and the whole system of his self- and mutual expectations. The stronger his sense of membership, the more reluctant will he be to restructure himself so radically. Thus the system of self- and mutual expectations from which these constraints and assurances proceed is powerful to sustain itself and therewith the social system that depends on it.

Between these two extremes of muting and containing conflict, the membership factor greatly enlarges the possibilities of *resolving* conflict.

Even a bargain is useless if neither party can be trusted to keep it. But the resolution of conflict does not depend merely on compromise or bargain within the limits of a given dispute, but on changing the parties' perception of the dispute itself. This is a function of mutual persuasion, a process which has received little attention from psychologists but one on which we should not spend so much time if we did not think it important.

Mutual Persuasion

Negotiators often go on talking even when there is apparently nothing to discuss, because they know from experience that communication sometimes produces changes which are important, even though they are hard to specify.

In any conflictual situation debate serves first to articulate the parties' views of the logistical constraints under which they are acting and the possibilities and costs of changing them. This helps to produce a more widely shared view of what the situation should be deemed to be and what can be done about it. And this may well include a more adequate view of the parties' own inter-relationship, in other contexts as well as in the context of the dispute.

It also changes or reinforces the way each party *values* the situation. Every debate on a conflictual situation appeals to criteria of value, as well as to threats and counter-threats; and these appeals, unless wholly disbelieved, affect the way in which each party pictures to itself the way the other party appreciates the situation. They may do more; they may affect—as they are intended to do—the criteria which each party accepts as relevant and the weight to be attached to it. There may thus result an appreciation more adequate and more commonly held.

This is reinforced by articulating what the parties expect of each other and what pressures they are prepared to bring to bear on each other. This brings to consciousness the second of the constraints already described; and this has some effect both on the willingness or potential coercers to coerce and of the others to be coerced. But it also makes clear and so confirms or varies how each party views and values its relation with the other, the restraints acknowledged by it and by the others and the assurances on which each can still rely.

Thus debate brings to consciousness and inevitably changes or confirms the self-expectations of the parties. Not only does each have to decide how far to acquiesce, how far and by what means to press its view, what action to take on the final decision. Even more importantly, it has to decide how its relation with the other party is to stand thereafter.

Thus all debates on conflictual issues are conducted at two levels. They are concerned not only with the matter at issue but also with the future relation of the parties as fellow members in that context and perhaps in many others. This second level of debate tends to grow more important as the debate proceeds and often ends by overshadowing the original issue. The constraints and assurances of membership may or may not contain the conflict over the specific issue. And if they do, the constraints and assurances of membership may be stronger or weaker in consequence. The second is usually by far the more important result.

The Threshold

This analysis seems to me to provide material for a better understanding of conflict and its management and particularly of that elusive threshold which is its particular subject. The argument so far can be summarised as follows:

1. Conflict is endemic in human affairs and its management is the most characteristically human function and skill.

2. The management of conflict includes and depends on containing it within the threshold beyond which it will become self-exciting and destructive of the *resources for resolving and containing conflict*.

3. This threshold is largely set by the constraints and assurances which the contestants feel as implicit in their common memberships.

4. These memberships are multiplying, as the systems in which people are organised (political, economic, social and other) become more numerous, more unstable and more interrelated.

5. All conflicts, whatever effect they may have on the conflictual situation, affect the relations of the parties in that and other contexts, notably by weakening or strengthening the constraints and assurances which they feel as implicit in their common memberships. So the management of conflict needs to be even more concerned with preserving these relationships than with the actual conflict.

6. This involves articulating a common appreciation of the multi-

ple objective relations which these subjective relations are required to support; but it is not achieved or maintained by that alone.

7. All human conflicts are both prosecuted and contained by communication at varying levels, from force and violence, through calculated falsification upwards to levels dependent on the highest levels of common appreciation and mutual trust. Bad communication, like bad currency, drives out the good; so the management of conflict is properly concerned with banning lower levels of communication so far as may be.

8. Coercion and deterrence, though legitimate and effective in limited fields, are low levels of communication, because they are inimical to the subjective constraints and assurances of membership, which are also the conditions for higher levels of communication and because threats are peculiarly liable to engender escalating conflict.

9. No authority is entitled to monopolise the loyalties of its members and no individual has the duty or the right to accord exclusive loyalty to any one of the systems to which he belongs. But equally no individual has the right to deny responsibility to his fellow members of *any* system to which he in fact belongs or to its common authority. The resultant conflict of loyalties is the most familiar example of that conflict which I have described as the essence of the human condition.

10. Total failure to meet this challenge results in the polarisation of conflict. At its extreme this results in the parties' loyalties becoming exclusively attached to one or other of two conflicting systems. When this occurs, the only duties felt to be owed or expected are owed to or expected from fellow members of a single system. All other persons, even the same persons in the context of a different membership, become alien, and probably enemy. For to be mutually dependent on those whom one does not trust and towards whom one feels no duty is an intolerable burden. So once the subjective constraints and assurances fail, the objective ones are potent to generate an overwhelming desire to cut loose from or destroy the entangling, threatening 'other'. Hence the peculiar virulence of civil wars, wars of secession and all such struggles.

This analysis prompts three reflections.

The management of conflict is not the responsibility of authority alone. It is the responsibility of every member of every system in all their endemic conflicts. The present tendency to regard authority as a precipitant, rather than a manager of conflict seems to me to be due partly to the fact that when conflict reaches what I described as its third level, authority does indeed become a protagonist, as the residuary legates of society's failure to resolve the conflict at an earlier stage. Even more, the tendency seems to me to be the pathological projection by individuals on to political authority of their own failure or refusal to face reality at the level at which they need to appreciate it, or to accept their own responsibliity for containing, if not resolving its conflicts.

Political authority is of course not free from the tendency of all authority to claim for its own system more autonomy than it can or should have; and it consequently needs to be constrained by other authorities, speaking for other systems, wider, narrower and overlapping. None the less political authorities, having general responsibility for regulating all relevant relations within their system, have usually a wider view than any functional authority and all but the most informed and mature individuals. Their officials, in my experience, appreciate conflictual situations more comprehensively, tolerate frustration more patiently and serve the common interest more devotedly than do most of their non-institutional critics. They thus give an example of a human approach to the management of conflict which those without such wide responsibilities might well follow and admire.

It would be vain to expect them all to do so; for a system so large and loosely integrated as a political state should not be regarded as composed of indistinguishable units. There will surely be some predators; some would-be destroyers; a variety of protesters, suffering varying degrees of alienation but with messages entitled to attention; and a body of assenting members, who will vary greatly in their capacity to attach reality to the wider implications of their memberships; in the strength of their sense of responsibility, loyalty and trust; and in the relative dominance of the systems which elicit these attitudes. It is the need and duty of every such society, despite these internal differences and weaknesses, to preserve the conditions in which the political dialogue can continue, by neutralising its enemies; and to do so it needs to use both organised authority and its own diffuse controls.

It seems to me impossible to hope for so subtle an exercise of power to preserve the conditions of freedom unless the relations of individuals and their other organisations to their organs of political authority become far more mutually responsive than they are now. The common factor in all the major revolutions of our time has been the need to make the individual more politically responsible than he has been in the past. Most of them have been more obviously successful at institutionalising the individual than at humanising their institutions. In any case solutions to political problems are not easily transferred from one culture to another. Answers are individual—but questions tend to be universal, none more so than the question how to manage conflict. One step towards answering it would be to accept the fact that institutionalised persons are at least as greatly needed as humanised institutions. By an institutional-ised person I mean one who accepts the constraints and assurances of membership in all the systems of which he forms part and there-with the responsibility for managing his share of the conflicts which they involve.

[Published in *Futures*, June 1972.]

CHAPTER 10

The Scope and Roles of the Educator

Today's children will grow up to face intellectual and ethical problems of immense difficulty, deriving from multiple membership. Already today each of us is dependent as never before on many human systems, some very large, some highly institutionalised, all making partly inconsistent demands on us for action or restraint as the necessary price of membership. A strike, for example, once a simple battle between employees and their employer for a larger share of his profits, now involves strikers and union officials, other unions and their members, non-unionised workers, an industry and several other industries, several departments of State, all political parties and the public at large; and every individual, concerned always in more than one capacity, needs to understand relations of great complexity and to make partly ethical judgments of great difficulty. The resultant conflicts, though sometimes muted, are often fiercer and always different because the contestants, however bitterly divided, are inescapably involved in each other's fate.

This disparity between the demands of multiple inter-dependence and the responses with which they are now met will be sharpened, perhaps unbearably, through the lifetimes of children now living, by all the constraints which are forcing the world to accept a steadier state. All the current distributive issues—between persons, classes and nations, between investment and consumption and between collective and individual use—will grow sharper, as growth in a finite system breeds its own limitations. Mounting conflict between rival land uses exemplifies a universal trend. And burgeoning information technology, while it may help policy makers, will increase the demands on the intelligence and the trust of the governed.

How far can formal education contribute to what today's children must learn, if they are to function adequately in tomorrow's world—or even in today's—as agents, as members and as persons? I believe we can arrive at a better answer than the one we are giving today if we review the current educational state with this dominant question constantly in mind.

The Educator's Responsibility

It is commonly regarded as useful today for business managers, Cabinet ministers and others engaged in purposeful activity to pause from time to time and ask themselves what they are trying to do and whether what they are doing is the best way to attain their ends. Teachers and educators have particular need to make such inquisitions and particular difficulty in making them. They are especially concerned to reckon the success of what they do in terms of its effect on other people, rather than on themselves. These others, the taught, are ill-placed to define their needs or even to insist in getting what they want. The more important results of education appear slowly and cumulatively and are not easily reversible. They are hard to identify. And they are to be judged at least partly by their success in fitting the taught to live in a world decades ahead which was never so unpredictable as now.

None the less—indeed, all the more—the attempt must be made. In this chapter I examine briefly the extent of the powers shared by educators and teachers and the corresponding extent of their responsibility; the matters of fact which they must assess as best they may and the matters of value on which they must commit themselves; the constraints under which they work; and the unique problem presented to them by the abundance of the present and the uncertainty of the future.

The responsibility for devising curricula, organising schools and colleges and actually teaching is widely distributed between the players of many different roles. To speak of them generally lacks precision; and so, still more, does any reference to teaching which covers the whole gamut of age for which education is arranged. These limitations I have to accept. I will use the word 'educators' to cover the whole of both ranges, unless I am referring particularly to those who actually teach.

Educators intervene in the development of other human beings to affect that development for the 'better'. They need to know or make assumptions about this process of development and the ways in which they can influence it. They need equally standards of what is better and what interventions are permissible in pursuit of it. The more they believe in the power of education, the more they need to believe in the rightness of what they are doing.

They work in conditions of great uncertainty. Young men and

women of 21 have reached that state of maturity from bundles of potentialities in cradles by a process of experience and reflection; and for anything from 11 to 16 of those 21 years part of that stream of experience has been designed to be educative. It is only a small part of the whole. Its effect on the taught is only partly distinguishable from effects produced by all the rest of their experience. But it is the field of the educators' responsibility and we should not spend so much time and money on it if we did not think it was very important. This is no less so if, as Professor Snyder[1] has shown to occur, its results are very different from what the educator designed or what the teacher thought he was teaching. Since educators must accept responsibility for what they do, however unintended, I shall regard as education only those effects but all those effects, whether intended or not, which flow from experiences designed to be educative.

These uncertainties are compounded today by two factors, both unique to our time. One is new only in degree. The amount of new knowledge, new ways of knowing and new situations needing to be understood has been increasing exponentially for many decades. This correspondingly increases the difficulty of the educator's task of choosing what to teach and of dealing with what is too important to ignore but too recent to understand. This difficulty is compounded by another which is new in kind. It becomes increasingly apparent that the future for which educators prepare the next generation will differ from the decades in which they have grown up, still more from earlier years, in ways more radical, yet more dependent on human judgment, than ever before. In consequence the task of the educator was never so important and never so controversial—and his ideas and practices in consequence never so much in need of review, though not necessarily of revision.

What can be done about these contemporary problems? I want first to explore some of the oddities of the educational process itself.

The Dimensions of Education

Even the intended effects of education are extraordinarily diverse. We need at least three words to distinguish them—skills, attitudes and knowledge. Each is a label for a bundle of disparates. Since knowledge is even more obscure than the others, I will leave it to the last.

We can distinguish at least four kinds of mental skill. Most basic are *expressive* skills, which enable the student to use all the languages available to him, verbal, mathematical, musical and graphical, among which verbal skills have a uniquely important place.

Associated with these are the *deductive* skills, which open to him all the processes of logical reasoning. These together make possible but do not fully account for the *appreciative* skills which underlie all forms of judgment. These skills enable us to represent to ourselves our manifold contexts and situations, actual and hypothetical, present and future and to judge them by a variety of standards which we develop in the process. I have described elsewhere[2] what I take to be the main features of this appreciative process and of the appreciative system which it generates in our heads and the standards which structure it. I conceive these as derived from the expectations which we develop of the natural world, of our fellows and of ourselves, three types of expectation which I have already distinguished. The models we thus build enable us to operate consciously on the world in which we suppose ourselves to be living and to change it, and our models, and even ourselves.

Beyond these appreciative skills are another group less easily defined which we may call *creative* skills. These are manifest in the creation or perception of novel forms and the questioning of familiar ones. They are, perhaps only a conspicuous extension of those *heuristic* skills which enter into all processes of appreciation.

If we understood better how the mind works, we might classify all these skills differently. Meantime these serve as convenient labels for skills which we recognise and value. They can all be learned in varying degrees and all to some extent taught, in that teachers can make it more (or less) probable that they will be learned. And all of them, regarded as skills, are generally agreed to be useful.

The category of learnable attitudes is even more elusive. It includes enjoyment in the exercise of our skills and interest in the subjects on which we exercise them; and the sense of obligation to bring our achievements, so far as we can, into line with our standards of excellence and propriety—standards which are also learned and therefore to some extent susceptible of teaching. This acknowledgment of the part played in human motivation by matching performance and experience with internally generated standards is a useful contribution which new ideas of communication and control are making to the impoverished field of motivation theory. I develop it a little further in the next chapter.

These skills and attitudes can only be developed in the pursuit of knowledge and they are equally needed for the pursuit of knowledge. They are transferable in varying degrees from one field of knowledge to another.

What then of knowledge? It too is an omnibus word which we can use of any representation which our skills enable us to make about the world we live in or our fellows or ourselves, in so far as we accept it with confidence for the purpose for which we produce it. We may need only to recall it from memory. We may create it by the skilful use of what we already know or can find out. It admits of subordinate categories of which I will briefly mention two.

The Natural and the Artificial.

Herbert Simon[3] in the book already noted recently reaffirmed a distinction—which is not new but has long been suspect—between natural science and what he called the sciences of the artificial. The subject of natural science is that part of the natural world which would be as it is if men were not here to think about it. But most of our environment, cultures and institutions as well as tools and buildings, is as it is because men have shaped it so. Simon asks what kind of *scientific* knowledge we can have about subject matter which might be other than it is. I am not concerned here to discuss his answer or to consider in any detail the long controversy to which it contributes. I mention it because educators, considering what they can and should teach and how best to teach it, need to distinguish between the different *kinds* of knowledge attainable in different *fields* of knowledge and the differences of skill involved in attaining them. The regularities of the artificial world are differently generated and differently sustained and the appreciation of them requires an understanding of human purposes and motivations. The laws of England are different from the laws of Nature in their character and their origin.

Knowledge of 'the artificial' can be arranged along a dimension according to the amount of human experience needed to understand it. The simplest tool, a hammer, for example, belongs to the domain of the artificial. But it would take little explanation to teach a child of almost any culture what a hammer *is*. Consider by contrast what is needed to understand what a bank *is*.

The outstanding success of the natural sciences and of the technologies based on them has had two effects of which educators need to take note. It has multiplied the demand for scientists and technologists and increased the educational importance of the relevant disciplines. It has also established the skills and knowledge of 'natural science' as typical of the skills and knowledge attainable by education and raised doubt about the status of any knowledge which is not 'scientific'.

Neither of these effects should be assumed to be permanent. The future is likely to demand skill in organising and managing the artificial environment far more than in manipulating the natural

F

one. So the skills needed to understand it will surely grow in importance by comparison with those based on natural science. Similarly the solution of human problems will *not*, I think, prove to be resolvable into the solution of scientific and technical problems. On the other hand, policy making at all levels will no doubt be increasingly penetrated by the new sciences and technologies of information, communication and control. Both those trends require educators to reassess the relevance of *all* the traditional disciplines to the needs of the next decades. And this seems to me to require that they marshal all they know or can assume about the spectrum of knowledge and skills corresponding to the expanding series of the knowable which stretches from the 'natural' into the ever more 'artificial'.

Experiential and Common Knowledge

This spectrum is more complex, I think, than Simon's simple dichotomy would suggest. At its more 'artificial' end, it requires us to distinguish between what I will call 'experiential' and 'common' knowledge.

Human life is known as a personal conscious experience. Language enables people to compare their personal and even their private conscious experiences, and the written word creates an inheritance of these records. The plays of Shakespeare, the philosophy of Locke, the novels of Tolstoy are personal communications. Even history is an historian's interpretation of human interaction, neither exhaustive nor necessarily contradicted by the different interpretation of another. Humanist education has always consisted largely in exposing each rising generation to what the previous generation thought best in this growing heritage of personal experience. The resulting knowledge may be called experiential knowledge and it accumulates on at least three levels. It shapes the learner's ideas of human relations and human experience and his standards of the way they should be. It also informs him of the way earlier generations have thought that human relations and experience were and should be, ideas which have been potent to shape their world. Finally it enables him to some extent to enter into the experience of other individuals *as agents* and as *experiencing persons* and thus influences what he expects of himself as an agent and as a person.

Experiential knowledge clearly differs in its character and its preconditions from the common knowledge which human observers accumulate about those parts of the natural and the artificial world which offer an independent field of reference composed of a few observable variables and which is not dependent on the variety of their personal experience. The difference is controversial; I shall enter the controversy only so far as to express my belief that experiential knowledge cannot, even in theory, be reduced to common knowledge but that, on the contrary, the world of the 'artificial' which surrounds us and includes us is created by and only understandable by experiential knowledge; that common knowledge is best regarded as a limiting, rather than a typical case of 'knowledge'.

In any case, educators need to take note of the important differences which I have roughly indicated between fields of knowledge and the corresponding kinds of knowledge and skills in knowing which mark progression along the dimension from the natural to the extremes of human artifice expressed in societies, cultures and, above all, human persons. For they are themselves artificers, concerned with the development of agents who are making themselves and therewith the 'artificial' world of tomorrow.

The Scope for the Educator

An old man looking back on life may legitimately regret either his failure to achieve various kinds of success, or the kinds and standards of success which he set himself to achieve, or both. And he may ask himself whether any difference in his education would have mitigated these failures. In so far as he rightly thinks it would, he has identified criteria by which to judge the aims or the effect of education, from the viewpoint of one of the taught.

His regrets can all, I think, be grouped in three classes—failure to act more effectively on his environment; failure to communicate better with his fellows; and failure in understanding and organising his own experience. The first includes all those aspects of life in which he can usefully be regarded as an agent acting on an environment—getting and keeping a job, managing money, acquiring and using power and so on. The second, an overlapping category, includes all those aspects of life in which he needs to be seen as a member of human social systems, familial, occupational, local, national or other, concerned with his relations with his fellow members and with the systems which claim his allegiance. The third, even more overlapping, covers the internal organisation of his own personality by which he makes himself and his experience sufficiently coherent and acceptable to be tolerable to himself, whether by integration and enlargement or by limitation and distortion. It views him as himself a system, capable in some degree of self-organisation in the interests of both stability and self-realisation.

All these fields are the proper concern of the educator. How far his influence can or should be exercised in any of them needs his careful consideration.

The individual's achievement in those three areas reflects his development, within his own biological limitations, under the impact of his own experience and reflection. This experience comes from three main sources—the course of events; the communications of other human beings; and the 'input' internally generated by his own reflection. Education (as I have defined it) contributes only part of the input, chiefly under the second head; and it plays today a novel role in a novel situation.

Throughout most of our history most children were taught specific work skills from an early age by those who were already practising them. Their skills in knowing about their physical environment, no less than in operating on it, came largely from this vocational training. Their skills in participating in the social systems of which they formed part (family, work group, local community, political community, class structure) were taught them by their fellow members and by the system's focus of authority, through the rewards and punishments attached to compliance and departure from what was expected of them in these roles. (In teaching these membership skills the work group was no less important than in teaching vocational skills.) Their personal development was guided partly by the norms established by their membership training and partly by the teaching of parents and of the Church.

All these sources of instruction are weaker than they were. Vocational training is hugely deferred; and when it comes, its content of membership training is often much less than it was. Membership training is weaker for lack of situations which make unequivocal demands on the young, as members, weakness partly due to the deferment of vocational training. Personal training is weaker by the impairment of membership training and the diminished authority of parents and of the church and of all possibly alternative authorities.

On the other hand, these traditional sources of instruction are supplemented far more than before by other non-educational inputs. The unending flow of oral comment and discussion by which they were always supplemented, was multiplied by the printed word in so far as the population became sufficiently literate to absorb its infinite variety. And today this is further multiplied by radio and television. Formal education adds only a small fraction to this gigantic input.

The educator, reflecting on these changes, will realise that he is being asked to do much that used to be done half-consciously by other institutions of society. He needs to decide how much of this demand he can usefully accept, having regard to his powers and his constraints.

He has two major fields of discretion. For several hours a day, perhaps through several years, he can choose to what the attention of the taught should be directed, what discretion to give them in choosing their fields of attention and how hard to drive them to produce measurable results. He also has some discretion during the same period in deciding how to structure the relationship of young people with each other and with a group of selected, trained adults and to determine what kinds of behaviour shall be praised, discouraged or treated as indifferent, what shall be expected of the taught and what they shall be taught to expect of themselves and each other. These powers are also educative. They are the main vehicle for that 'hidden curriculum' which Professor Snyder has distinguished in the book already mentioned.

The two fields are connected. Group projects, for example, have ancillary effects different from those of individual projects. Individual competitiveness, encouraged as a spur to individual learning, is also a social determinant. None the less, the two fields are distinct and partly complementary. For some purposes even small classes, still more large ones, are the regrettable dilution of teaching skills which would be ideally directed to a single child. For other purposes the tutor of a single child would have to leave to others much that the organisers of a school can themselves arrange. For yet others nothing may equal the impersonal monitoring of a teaching machine.

In any case, the structuring of relationships and standards of relating, no less than the choice of curriculum, is part of the educator's field of discretion.

The educator exercises these discretions under enormous constraints. The nature of his task as now conceived (and to some extent inescapably) restricts him in the extent to which he can devise learning situations other than the engagement of individuals with books. The children he teaches are diverse in their genetic endowment and in their cultural background. These diversities give them very different capacities and tolerances for this kind of learning situation; and the more egalitarian the educational system, the more these inequalities complicate his task of communication. He is himself part of an educational sub-culture which generates its own standards of success and discourages innovation which runs counter to these standards. And the standards are to some extent self-validating; success in learning what the educator teaches, is success even though it is no evidence in itself of the aptitude of what was taught. He controls a much smaller part than formerly of the cultural input of his charges. He is weakly placed to integrate an incoherent culture.

The Roles of the Educator

None the less the educator's role is important in all the three fields which I have distinguished and which I will label as the development of the individual as agent, as member and as person. It is a multiple role. He clearly has a major role (A) in teaching the basic mental skills, including literacy and numeracy, which his society assumes that *all* its members will possess. He has some further role (B) in equipping the young to appreciate the situations in which they will find themselves; and (C) in teaching them, partly by actual experience, the standards and elementary techniques of membership which they will need in all their membership relations, whether as citizens, employees or otherwise. This includes the ability to criticise the systems of which they form part with the responsibility of members and to reconcile the conflicts inherent in multiple membership. He has some role (D) in encouraging each of them to develop his or her natural endowments irrespective of their relevance to vocational or membership needs. He has a growing role (E) in supplying the educational content of vocational training, which cannot be learned 'on the job'. He has a wider general role (F) as guardian and transmitter of the educational heritage; and at the extremities of higher education he has the further role (G) of extending knowledge and devising new skills. And viewed as a whole, the educational sub-culture has the further roles (H) of supplying academic skills increasingly demanded by government and industry and (I) of criticising the culture whose transmission it is mediating.

I can do no more than mention most of these roles but I will add a few comments on some of them.

Role A raises some important technical questions. How best can the expressive and deductive skills, notably language and calculation, be taught and at what ages? It is important not to miss times in biological development when skills can most easily be learned and equally not to try to teach too early skills for which today later opportunities for learning can be devised.

Even more important and much more difficult is the question—what *are* the skills and bodies of knowledge which today's citizens need to have and what should be the educational contribution to them? This involves roles B and C. The field of knowledge includes the complex system of systems which supports all its members and the skills include the skills which its members need as members;

not least, the critical skills which mediate change from within. Here again, important questions of timing arise.

The institutions, public and private, of a modern state are the all-embracing environment of each individual. Yet they are not apparent to him or adequately taught at present by the natural course of communication and experience. A much larger quotient than ever before needs, I believe, to be specifically taught, as the present phase of a continuing historical process of which later phases will concern the young as adult members and agents. The significance of past phases, even if taught, will be largely lost if they are not seen in their historical relevance to the present. Such teaching may be difficult at times of rapid and controversial change. It remains, I think, a valid expectation that children emerging as adults into an institutional milieu should have been taught whatever skills and knowledge education can give them to understand it and its demands.

These are not inconsistent with the self-development which it is also the educator's role (D) to encourage. The antithesis between development as member and as person, so common today, is perhaps the most pathological symptom of our age. It is no less significant for that. Schools and colleges can do something to sharpen or abate it, largely through their 'hidden curriculum'.

No sharp line divides the education of the individual generally as agent from his preparation for a specific vocation. None the less vocational demands for education beyond training 'on the job' complicate the educator's problem both by the amount of time they claim and by the type and amount of specialism which they involve.

The amount of time and hence the difficulty of the problem vary very much with the amount of technology involved in the vocation. Most lawyers can leave their vocational education until after their first degree. Would-be doctors and engineers must begin to take account of it in their schooldays. The growth of information technology is likely to increase the load and make it more universal.

More subtle is the impact of vocational training on the *level* of study. Educators are bound to teach all subjects at two—even three—levels. Their role (F) as guardians and transmitters of the intellectual heritage and (G) their duty to extend their discipline, with its ancillary obligation (role E again) to produce teachers competent to take their own places, compel them to teach every subject in depth. But they are equally required (roles A, B and C) to teach their subjects at a level appropriate to laymen. Future practitioners of vocations other than teaching need yet another level. What a layman needs to know about, say, physics differs from the needs of a future teacher of physics and also from those of most engineers; and simpler needs can seldom be met by partial contact with a curriculum designed for future adepts.

The academic quotient of vocational training, in so far as it is separable from general education, would seem to be best taught in close association with in-service training, so that students can relate it to a work situation with which they are already identified. The last 25 years in Britain have seen a great increase in the academic content of in-service training, both in early and in later years; notably in management courses for men in mid-career and in the part-time and 'sandwich' courses which lead so many young workers in Britain, through 'National' certificates, to professional membership of institutions of engineering and some other vocations. It may be that, as education comes to be more largely extended into adult life, so work experience will be injected earlier into the life of the student. There will surely remain, however, the problem of sustaining most of the young through many years of whole-time study before they enter on a vocation.

There is conflict between the needs of general and vocational education, and also between general and specialist education. There is conflict between the demand for testable skills and knowledge and for less testable but more fundamental skills and attitudes. Subjects compete, like budget headings, for scarce time and attention. There is some conflict between the demands of the overt and the hidden curriculum, in that the best way to teach the second is not always the quickest way to teach the first. There is conflict between skills and knowledge needed to understand the 'natural' world, teachable, testable, uncontroversial and embarrassing only by their volume, and those other skills and knowledge needed to understand the 'artificial' world, elusive, controversial, hard to teach but infinitely more important. There is some conflict between the disparate values of experiential and common knowledge.

There is some conflict between the role of the educational subculture as a supplier of intellectual services to government and business and its role as critic of the culture which it mediates.

These are among the conflicts which it is the educator's professional task to resolve or contain. Like any other professional, he is neither a dictator nor a slave. It is his professional duty to keep in view, both in what he teaches and in how he teaches it, the educational purposes implicit in his multiple role. And this he can contribute in his partnership with the vocations in their vocational training, no less than in the most 'general' education. As I have already argued, the playing of vocational roles is as human an exercise as any other.

What then of the alleged conflict, so much feared, between the needs of the individual and those of society or, worse, 'the State'? Our century has seen monstrous perversions of whole generations by the exercise of state power in this formative field. Yet it seems to me to be at this moment the least of the anxieties which need worry an educator in the Western world. This is partly because I believe that the power of totalitarian régimes to condition their populations depends far more on their actions in inhibiting the expression of dissent than in the one-sided influence of what they teach. It springs also from a judgment of the historical situation. There have been times when the overriding demands of society have inhibited individual development, sometimes so much as to seal off the sources of innovation and render the society itself impotent for change. But that is not the plight of Western society today. Doubt and dissent never had so free a run; dissent is limited only by lack of an orthodoxy from which to deviate. The individual suffers not from the overweening demands of a single membership but from the inability of *all* the systems on which he depends to elicit from or offer to their members the constraints and assurances of membership. Since this is also the main danger which threatens every human system, not least the State, the present needs of State and individual, as it seems to me, have seldom been so congruent.

The educator, reviewing the situation relevant to him as an educator, will identify at least three fields of uncertain fact. One comprises the biological factors of the learning process, which define its possibilities, its limitations and its individual variety. A second comprises the socio-cultural facts which define the educator's scope and the streams of competing input. A third includes the facts about 'future history'—those assumptions about the world in which today's young will live as adults, which affect the preparation they should have now.

He will also identify at least three fields of relevant value judgment, corresponding to the three fields of experience I distinguished earlier. One concerns the knowledge, skills and attitudes which will be most needed to survive and prosper in that anticipated world. A second concerns the requirements of membership in its manifold social systems. A third concerns the requirements of personal growth and integrity in such a world.

The three conflict to some extent and each group has its inner conflicts. For the educator the conflicts are accentuated by the fact that he must use such discretion as he has to choose for others, rather than for himself. His problem is not on that account either insoluble or unique. Criteria of value always conflict. To resolve or contain their conflicts is the basic responsibility of human life. It always affects other people.

He is not required to choose *in vacuo*. He has the guidance of a huge tradition, the noblest artifact yet achieved by man. He has the constraints inherent in his ignorance, his weakness and his place in the many-sided dialogue through which alone he can innovate. Within these limitations he has to make the unique contribution possible from one whose concern and criterion of relevance is to fit the young, as agents, as members and as persons, for a future which, whatever its strangeness, will surely set those same problems which life has always set to those whose ambition it is to live neither as 'yes-men' nor as 'no-men' but as men.

[Based on an article published in the *Journal of Curriculum Studies*.]

Notes and References
1. Benson R. Snyder, *The Hidden Curriculum,* 1970. Cambridge, Mass. The M.I.T. Press.
2. E.g. in *The Art of Judgment,* 1965. Chapman & Hall and Basic Books also Methuen University Paperbacks, and *Value Systems and Social Process,* 1968. Tavistock Publications and Basic Books, also Penguin Books.
3. Herbert Simon, *The Sciences of the Artificial,* 1969, Cambridge, Mass. The M.I.T. Press.

CHAPTER 11

Values, Norms and Policies

A Definition of Norms

In his book, *Technological Planning and Social Futures*, Dr Erich Jantsch[1] provides a diagram showing the sequence of mental operations which lead from policy making through planning and decision making to rational creative action. Policies precede strategies. Strategies precede tactics. But policies occupy not the top level but the third level of his diagram. Above the policy level come two levels labelled Values and Norms, with mutual interactions shown between values, norms and policies. Unlike some writers in this field, Dr Jantsch does not take 'goals' for granted. Values and norms bombard the policy maker with multiple disparities between the course of events as it is and is likely to be and its course as he would wish it to be. These signals often mutually conflict and their demands always far exceed what he can achieve. It is his job to choose and realise one among the many possible partial solutions of this intrinsically insoluble problem. And if he understands his function as well as he should, he knows that his solution can and should be only temporary, since its successes as well as its failures will set new problems for his successors. On the other hand his solution must last long enough to realise its own promise and pave the way for what will follow.

Though many—not all—writers on policy making would agree in general with this statement, few if any have addressed themselves primarily to elucidating the relations between values, norms and policies or even the meanings of these terms. The reasons are obvious but the result is none the less disastrous. Values and norms, as I shall seek to show, are terms of unusable vagueness today, not because they cannot be usefully defined, but because they have not yet been sufficiently analysed, although an abundant store of accessible fact is available for the purpose.

This chapter is a contribution towards filling this gap.

Although policy making is common to public and business affairs and indeed to the management of all human affairs, it is liable to be over-simplified in the study of business decisions in a way which is impossible in the public sector. So it is convenient to choose an example from the field of social policy.

A century ago most homes in Britain had a well in the garden, a privy in the garden and a tank to catch the rain water. Much of the washing was done with rain water, being soft and (then) clean. The well supplied the rest, including the drinking water. The slops and the excrement went on to the garden, either directly or through the compost heap. The generation, use and disposal of water was contained in an area no larger than the site of a cottage. Human waste was disposed of by a separate system, equally small and self-contained.

Today the universal use of water to dispose of sewage has linked the two systems and each combined system covers an area which in Britain is at least as large as the largest river's catchment area and will soon be much larger. The factual inter-dependence of people in the matter of water and sewage has hugely proliferated. So have their expectations of the system, of each other and of themselves. It is today regarded as 'unacceptable' that even an isolated home should lack indoor sanitation and an indoor water supply. In the debate on social policy and its priorities 'bad housing' bulks large; and among its constituents the standards of water supply and sanitation have an important place. Other criteria, such as the ratio of persons to rooms, have similar levels which define the unacceptable. Houses which fail to satisfy current standards of the acceptable are 'sub-standard'. Even policy makers who do not respond to pressure to bring houses up to standard seldom venture to deny that such standards exist and are valid today, even though they were different or even absent a century ago.

Standards of this kind provide the structure of social policy; countless other examples suggest themselves. They illustrate a very common form of mental operation. Some state of affairs, actual or hypothetical, is compared with a standard of what ought to be and is found not to 'fit'. In cybernetic terms a mis-match signal is generated. The agent who makes this judgment may for the moment be unable to do anything to remedy the disparity or he may be unwilling to do what he might because some other mis-match is claiming his resources and his attention. None the less the signal has been generated and will in time have its effect on policy.

Standards of this kind are what I think should be meant by norms. They are concrete, specific and—tacit. They reveal themselves only by the signals of match or mis-match which they generate when they are evoked by specific cases. They may indeed be made explicit in formal rules and regulations. But these also are only effective when applied to specific cases; and, once formalised, they are liable to diverge increasingly from the developing tacit norm which they try to express.

Tacit norms are common. We tend to overlook them, because we are conditioned to ignore the tacit aspects of our thinking, unless they appear to be pathological. Christopher Alexander[2] in a book primarily devoted to physical design, says in effect that the designer's task is to 'eliminate misfit', rather than to create form, which is a tacit standard knowable only through the agreeable abatement of mis-match signals which mark the designer's approach to it. And in support of his argument that norms are necessarily tacit, he cites the difficulty of doctors in defining health and of psychiatrists in defining psychological normality.

Clearly nothing is more important to mankind than the process by which these tacit norms develop. This process, though complex, is familiar and is more easily studied in a social than in an individual context. To return to the example already given, the standards of the single dwelling, self-contained for water and sewage, had long been changing in towns through simple pressures of density. In England in mid-19th century the inconvenience of density was amplified by increased consciousness of the attendant health hazard. Cities have always been prone to epidemics and plagues; but by mid-19th century dawning understanding of the possibility of *controlling* disease began to generate standards of acceptability regarding those factors which were recognised as contributing to health. Amongst these were the supply of pure water and the disposal of human excrement.

A host of diverse factors sped the change. The promise of a market for pipes of all sizes encouraged the production of the necessary hardware. The convenience of indoor water and sanitation attracted the rich and made the bathroom a status symbol. Soon its absence became a negative status symbol, which began to offend sensitive consciences. Widening political suffrage made the poor more influential. Growing concern for equality and social justice made those who felt it readier to measure the deficiencies of the poor against standards once peculiar to the rich. Both of the two influences last mentioned helped to determine who stood for election in local government, what they proposed and to what standards they appealed.

In this familiar mixture of motives and pressures two critically important trends can be discerned. One is the transition of some state of affairs from the status of 'act of God' to the status of 'act of man'. Toil, inconvenience, sickness and death have always been part of the human condition. But in the past century in the West, far more than at any other place or time, aspects of this condition have been distinguished as something which could and should be controlled by men.

Once this happens, the burden and its distribution become a matter of public policy about which it is relevant to argue that it *ought to be* other than it is. It is judged by the sort of expectation that we entertain not of the natural world but of the human world— to use against the distinction which Herbert Simon recently drew between what is as it is, independent of man's design and what owes its form partly to human artifice. What men might shape otherwise allows and invites *ethical* criteria.

The other trend is the continual re-adjustment of the standard thus set by all the influences illustrated by my example. The standard may be more or less agreed. It may go down rather than up. But only a political cataclysm is likely to relegate it again to the field of the uncontrollable.

Norms and Values

Among the many factors constantly at work to change the setting of these tacit norms, one is explicit mutual persuasion. Textbooks of psychology have very little to say about the process by which concerned people persuade others to share their concerns merely by talking to them. But it is a matter of common experience that they do so; and we should hardly devote so much time to the process if we did not think it important. For example, although many factors prepared the way for the elimination of slavery in the 19th century, few people would be satisfied with an account that did not mention Wilberforce.

The debate on social policy is full of appeals to concepts such as equality, justice and liberty. These are abstract words of great ambiguity and imprecision. Therein lies their power and their value. Freedom, for example, deserves and needs to be discussed in every generation precisely because every generation needs to re-define its content. This it could not do if the word were not open-ended, a classification constantly growing and changing with use.

Another reason why these abstract qualitative words deserve endless debate is that they come in complementary and partly inconsistent pairs, such as freedom and order, independence and inter-dependence, equality and self-development, justice and mercy. Each member of a pair is a compendious label for a number of 'values' more or less inconsistent with those implied by the other, as well as being the contradiction of its own opposite. They thus supply an indispensable means to discuss the always conflicting and disparate costs and benefits which can be anticipated as likely to flow from any deliberate human intervention in the course of affairs.

These explicit abstract terms refer to what I think should be regarded as values. They contrast strikingly with norms in several ways. Values are general and explicit. Norms are specific and tacit. Yet each affects the other and both change in the course of the process already illustrated.

That values affect norms is the faith behind all attempts at mutual persuasion and the experience which sustains them. But norms equally affect and even generate the values to which they appeal. Wilberforce could attack slavery in the name of freedom, justice and equality and these appeals helped to change in more lethargic or insensitive minds the tacit standards of what they should find unacceptable in the actual laws and practices of their day and age. But these tacit standards had been and would still be the source from which the abstract values gained their emotive power.

Freedom had been a potent word for centuries in earlier ages, which accepted slavery as a human condition. But its content had been different. The anti-slavery campaign enlarged it in ways which would not easily be undone. Similarly reformers today, urging higher priority for providing everyone with a home of 'acceptable' standard, appeal to the same explicit general values. But the standards of what is acceptable have risen, giving a new content to those generalities. And the new content will play a part in changing still further the current tacit standards. This is precisely the object of the reformers' explicit persuasion.

The meanings which I have given to norms and values, though still imprecise, seem to me a useful step towards distinguishing them and understanding their mutual relationships. It also makes clear the inconsistencies inherent in each.

I have already described those inherent in 'paired' values. Our tacit norms equally lack inherent consistency. The mis-match generated by unacceptable housing invites action which will mitigate it; but any possible action, when examined, may well generate equally intense mis-match signals by comparison with some other norm and may be rejected at first, for long or even indefinitely, on appeal to the same on other values. And the signal itself must compete for attention with many other mis-match signals, equally valid, all competing for limited resources, often also competing with each other in that any action to abate one will intensify another.

Thus neither our tacit norms nor our explicit values is a stable system. Perhaps it never should be. Certainly neither was ever so unstable as now for two reasons already given. Increasing human power over the natural environment focuses human expectations on what man should do rather than on what nature will do and thus hugely expands the ethical dimension. And the response of authority to these expectations speeds the rate at which they grow.

This then is the situation in which the policy maker works. It is for him to choose some attainable mix of the disparate benefits and costs with which the current label of 'mis-match' requires him to deal. He *must* reject some of these requirements. What he rejects, no less than what he accepts, will influence the future setting of the norms and values of his society. And his actions will influence them no less through their successes than through their failures.

The Beveridge report and its resultant legislation in Britain is a good example of this threefold interaction. The report identified five 'giant evils'—unemployment, sickness, ignorance, squalor and want. The dramatic language is significant. Giants, in folklore, are not only strong and bad, but also vulnerable. A hero comes who does not accept them as part of the natural order. He kills them. The report invited its readers to regard these age-old human conditions as equally defeasible. All were already under some attack, but the legislation based on the Beveridge report expressed a new sense of what was unacceptable and a new determination to alter it.

Twenty-five years later the situation is different. So are the levels of the tacit norms and the contents of the explicit values. A new Beveridge report might identify some new giants. Among the agencies which have changed the situation, the norms and the values, a major one has been the report itself and the stream of policy making which it has stimulated and influenced.

Policies and Policy Makers

This then is what I conceive to be the distinction between norms and values, the relations between them and the mutual relation between them and the policies which give them partial expression. What does all this tell us about the role of the policy maker and the abilities which we implicitly attribute to him?

The policy maker is subject to constraints, which limit what he can do—or what he thinks he can do. The distinction is important. If he attempts what he cannot achieve, events will constrain him. If, on the other hand, he does not attempt something because he estimates that it is impossible or too costly or too risky, he is constrained by his own appreciation of the situation. Since it is usually disastrous to go blindly on until we are powerless to go further, the second is, or ought to be, the more normal form of constraint. None the less, those who accept such constraints can never *prove*, even after the event, that if they had ignored them, they would in fact have suffered the disasters which they anticipated.

Such constraints may derive from an appreciation of circumstances wholly beyond the policy maker's control. More often, they are beyond his control only because his own decisions have made them so. Where they derive from lack of resources, this could often be made good, if he were willing to divert resources earmarked for other purposes. Where they derive from resistance or lack of support among those whose assent or support would be needed, these attitudes could often be changed, quickly or slowly, by bargain, threat or persuasion. Only in the limiting case, usually rare, are these constraints wholly independent of his own action and his own judgment.

These constraints can usefully be classified in another way. Some are imposed by his expectation of the course of events. Some are imposed by his expectations of other people and especially by his knowledge of what they expect of him. Yet others are imposed by what he has come to expect of himself. The distinction between these three is important and often overlooked.

Human beings often tell each other what they want each other to do. The wish may be expressed as a command or as a request or as a piece of information which has obvious implications for action. It may or may not elicit the desired response. But whether it does so or not, it is a communication different in kind from those which we derive from observing the natural world. And whether the recipient complies or not, his response has an effect on the human sender which has no counterpart in our relations with the natural world.

Moreover, such express communications supplement and depend on a much larger set of assumptions about the tacit norms and explicit values of those with whom we are in communication. This tissue of mutual expectations is what structures the human world and makes human communication possible.

The policy maker, surveying the constraints which other people's expectations place upon his freedom of decision and action, is estimating the way they will judge and respond to the various actions and ways of action which are open to him. But he need not accept these as independent variables, as he would accept the laws of the natural world. They may be abated or intensified by what he does, even by the way he does it, because they are responsive to human communication; and between human beings all acts are also communications. The domain in which people persuade, bargain or even coerce each other has its own distinctive laws, the laws of communication, which operate at many levels. As already mentioned, even the bomb at Hiroshima was, and was intended to be, more effective as a communication than as an agent of destruction. Much higher levels than bombs are possible and necessary in making and implementing policy.

Apart from constraints, the policy maker is also conscious of pressures, identical in origin with the corresponding constraints. Some are inherent in the logic of events. Dominant among these is the need to preserve the stability of the system which it is his function to regulate, a condition, though by no means an adequate criterion, of his success as a policy maker. Some come from pressure groups of his constituents, and others who are concerned with his policies and able to exert some influence upon him. These pressures always conflict with each other and often conflict with what would otherwise be the course of his policy, even with what seems to him the logic of event.

It is sometimes supposed that the policy maker is no more than a broker among these conflicting pressures, concerned only to find a viable compromise between them within the overall limitations imposed by his constraints. Even if policy were no more than this, it would put a premium on high levels of rare skills. The policy maker would need to be adept at working out the logical implications of alternative possible actions, and ingenious in devising novel courses which would better combine diverse benefits and minimise unacceptable costs. I will call these logical skills and heuristic skills. He would also need persuasive skills, to get others to share his insights. Few people combine these skills in an outstanding degree, so good policy makers, even at this level, are likely to be rare.

Yet although much policy making is no more than brokerage between competing constraints and pressures, no policy maker should confine himself to this role. He has his own norms and values, never quite the same in character or level as those which move the pressurisers and the containers. He has the right and the duty to advocate them. And his advocacy will surely make a difference, dissolving resistance, polarising resistance or both.

So the policy maker, whatever the level at which he operates, is also an artist in the creation of coherent and viable form in human behaviour; and, like any other artist, he must believe in the goodness, as well as the coherence and viability of the design which he is trying to realise. And even beyond this, he is an artist in shaping the norms and values from which his policy is made. For he affects these both directly by advocating his policies and indirectly through his policies when they are in operation.

He thus has scope for initiation and for creation. So have we all. It is what we should expect in a human communication system in which every factor is a function of all the others. But the policy maker's role magnifies this scope and makes him more than usually potent for good and ill.

Some Implications

This analysis may seem to imply a view of human motivation more complex than is currently fashionable. It is not, however, more complex than we all use in common speech. The distinctions which I have drawn are reflected in four common verbs. What we want and do not want to do is limited and often transformed not only by what we can and cannot do, but also by what we must and must not do, where those words are used of social obligation in the widest sense, and also by what we ought and ought not to do, where those words cover at least those expectations which we have developed of ourselves. Thus, in the example already given, the last century has seen a change in what people want in the matter of sewage and water supply; a change in what they can have and in what they actually enjoy; and changes in what they expect of their institutions, of each other and of themselves. It would be strange if the verbs which distinguish these changes did not correspond with some psychological realities. If these need detailed justification, they require an exposition more elaborate than could be added to this paper. But it may help to make the argument clearer if I summarise the levels of control of human behaviour which are here implied.

It is abundantly clear that animal behaviour is subject to a hierarchy of controls which often conflict, and that human behaviour derives its greater coherence from higher levels of organisation, which have their own costs and ultimately their own limits in the greater conflicts which they engender. (This contrast will become apparent to anyone who compares his own behaviour in his more human moments, with that of a bird on a bird table.) I find it useful to distinguish five main levels.

The lowest is the level of innate response. I will call it the level of 'control by releaser', since the study of it has shown that response is a function of the state of the organism, as well as of the environment. This level is constantly qualified by the second level, which is the level of conditioned response, and which has also been exhaustively studied. Conditioned responses frequently conflict with each other, as well as with the level below. I will call this level 'control by rule', since its formula is—'In these circumstances, do this', where the 'circumstances' may range from a simple signal to any complex of event sufficiently characterised to be recognisable.

When the agent develops any capacity for recognising causal relations and for modelling the future course of events on various hypotheses, simpler controls are further modified. The expected *result* of the intended activity becomes potent to evoke or inhibit action. I will call this level 'control by purpose'. The new logical and heuristic powers on which it depends are just visible at levels below the human, but both attain in man levels so outstanding that purposeful behaviour has become the paradigm of rational action. Whilst these logical and heuristic powers increase the range of possible coherent action, they equally increase its inherent motivational conflict. For control by purpose not only conflicts constantly with control by rule (still very strong in all of us) but also breeds endless internal conflicts of its own, as it uncovers ever more inconsistent and disparate costs and benefits, flowing from an ever wider repertory of conceivable actions.

But these three levels do not encompass the whole of what men manifestly do. No ingenuity of logical or heuristic process can of itself explain why the agent chooses one course rather than another. For this we must postulate criteria and make assumptions about their origin, development and relevant strength and cogency. In doing so we credit the agent with power to respond to a new and more refined sort of signal, though one no longer unfamiliar, since it is a common feature of all man-made control mechanisms. These are signals internally generated by comparing the course of event, actual or hypothetical, with standards present in his mind, and acting on the signals of match or mis-match which the comparison generates. Such signals are different from those which operate control by rule and are a necessary supplement to those which operate control by purpose. Now that science has legitimised such signals, we can allow ourselves to see them throughout the human scene. It is no longer necessary to stretch the concept of tension reduction to breaking point and beyond to account for the human tendency to preserve match and abate mis-match signals. It is not even necessary to postulate a 'drive' to account for this familiar behaviour. The concept of motivation itself, with its out-moded implication that form depends on energy, gives way at this level to the more comprehensive and appropriate concept of control by standard or norm.

Once again, the potential increase in coherence is bought at the price of increasing conflict. For standards conflict with each other and obedience to them frequently frustrates specific purposes. These stresses, however, are likely to find acceptable solutions, so long as the standards remain relatively constant. Even so, their slow change with time, visible in the course of history, invites the question how they develop and how those who obey them can also be those who change them. This problem was an unsolved intellectual scandal within living memory even in the field in which it is most visible and has been most studied, namely the growth of the common law. But as the rate of other changes quickens, whilst the rate at which the generations change becomes if anything slower, the need to change the standards we live by even while we use them, becomes ever more important and ever more threatening. The function of resetting norms and values becomes a conscious one. And with it we can discern a new level of control, a level of collective self-control or self-determination which casts special responsibility on the policy maker.

These five levels of control are summarised in the table on the next page. They are a crude and over-simplified approach to a familiar story of development. I hope that further study will soon refine them out of all recognition. I feel only one confident assurance about them. They will not be 'reduced' by one of those 'nothing but' hypotheses so dear to some scientists when they approach the human realm. The fourth and fifth levels will not be dissolved into the second and third—unless, of course, human life itself is so dissolved.

In that case, we shall no longer study the more important aspects of policy making.

A summary of Five Levels of Control.

Level 1. CONTROL BY RELEASER
The realm of innate response qualified by

Level 2. CONTROL BY RULE
The realm of conditioned response, amplified as logical and heuristic powers develop, to create the often conflicting level of

Level 3. CONTROL BY PURPOSE
The realm of know how, generating a volume and variety of choice which is unmanageable without

Level 4. CONTROL BY NORM
Comparison by match and mis-match signals generated by hypothetical as well as actual courses of events with tacit standards which define their acceptability. This level breaks down so soon as norms cease to be relatively stable and universally held unless it is supported by

Level 5. CONTROL BY SELF-DETERMINATION
A process both individual and social which depends essentially on ethical debate and reflection about changing norms and values and on the policy making which both expresses and generates that debate. It is neither more nor less 'rational' than the process already described which has fixed the current standard of an acceptable British house.

[published in *Policy Sciences*, Vol. 4, No. 1, March 1973]

Notes and References

1. Erich Jantsch. Technological Planning and Social Futures. 1972. London. Associated Business Programmes Ltd., p. 16.
2. Christopher Alexander—Notes on the Synthesis of Form. 1967. Harvard University Press.

Index